Techniques of Twentieth Century Composition

A Guide to the Materials of Modern Music

Techniques of
Twentieth Century
Composition

A Guide to the Materials

of Modern Music

Leon Dallin
California State University
Long Beach

Third Edition

WM. C. BROWN COMPANY PUBLISHERS
Dubuque, Iowa

MUSIC SERIES

Consulting Editor
Frederick W. Westphal
California State University, Sacramento

Printed in the United States of America

To those who made this book possible—
my teachers, my students, my colleagues,
and most especially my wife,
who is the real writer in the family.

Contents

Preface

T HE training of musicians no longer begins with the music of the eighteenth century and ends with that of the nineteenth century. Older and newer music deserve and are receiving added emphasis in colleges, universities, and schools of music. This book is devoted to the music of the twentieth century.

The approach is appropriate for composers exploring contemporary idioms, for performers learning to cope with the innovations of modern music, and for teachers developing their understanding and appreciation of the music of our time. All three categories are served by this text. It is designed to provide essential knowledge of the techniques and materials of twentieth-century music and to bridge the gulf between traditional academic training and current practice.

Courses in harmony and counterpoint are prescribed for prospective composers, performers, and teachers alike. The study of composition is a logical and necessary continuation. In conventional idioms technical proficiency and artistic discrimination are acquired, after familiarity through listening and performing, by analyzing and writing. Using this approach for modern music accomplishes the same purposes and reveals the functional relationships between antiquated resources and their contemporary counterparts. Systematic utilization of new materials in creative exercises teaches composers to write the musical language of our time, performers to speak it, and listeners to understand it. The individuality of composers is asserted by the choices they make from the infinite possibilities when they are deliberately imitating established styles. Besides, individuality is not so much something to strive for as something which emerges spontaneously with maturity and technical proficiency. Performers and teachers turn to their particular specialties before reaching this level of attainment, but their musical insight is immeasurably enriched by temporarily assuming the role of the composer.

The techniques and materials of twentieth-century music are surveyed and illustrated with more than 300 examples drawn exclusively from the works of recognized composers. The coverage is comprehensive, and all significant styles and procedures are represented. The sources of the examples are identified by composer, title, page or movement, date, and publisher, and recordings not listed in the *Schwann Record and Tape Guides* are specified. To facilitate the reading of the examples by less experienced musicians and to make them readily playable on the piano, the treble and bass clefs are used. Orchestral scores have been transposed and reduced, with few exceptions, and unessential elements have been omitted. Contemporary devices with direct antecedents in the music of the past are explained using conventional terminology and symbols. The components of complex sonorities, for example, are arranged on the staff to reveal their underlying structures, obviating the need for a new system of analysis.

The present volume evolved from efforts extending back to the 1940s to develop a logical and systematic presentation of the techniques and materials of twentieth-century music to classes in composition and theory. Teachers who have specialized in other areas of music and composers who are more interested in creating new works than in organizing and systematizing their knowledge for the benefit of students should find it equally useful as a text. I wish to express my appreciation to the students who inspired and tested the original edition and to the teachers whose suggestions contributed to the present edition and whose adoptions made it possible. I also wish to thank the composers and publishers who generously granted permission to quote from copyrighted works.

Leon Dallin

Suggestions for the Use of This Book

THE examples constitute a vital feature of this text. They are taken from works for which scores and/or recordings are generally available. Page numbers for the examples refer to their location in the edition indicated, if any; otherwise in the Kalmus[1] score. Dates other than in the copyright notices are approximate dates of composition, publication, or first performance. Recordings of works not listed under the composer's name in the *Schwann Record and Tape Guides* are identified. The musical examples in the text, or better still the works from which they are taken, should be studied and played in class or as outside assignments. Comments in the text are focused on the subject of the particular chapter, but other aspects of the examples can be considered as they arise in the process of classroom discussion. When the examples are observed in context and heard in the original medium, the techniques illustrated are perceived as elements of style, and their contribution to musical values can be assessed. Systematic exposure to the broad spectrum of twentieth-century music represented in the text is essential if musicians are to understand, perform, and appreciate properly the music of our time.

The techniques and materials examined are in general use, and much is to be gained by searching out additional examples similar to those printed in the book. Alert performers and perceptive listeners will strive continually to identify and assimilate the twentieth-century practices to which they are exposed in their various musical activities.

The expectation is not that all types of modern music will be found equally attractive, but to make cogent evaluations and to produce mature compositions, all must be familiar. It is preferable to explore every phase of contemporary composition, however briefly, than to concentrate on one to the exclusion of another. The relative amount of time spent in listening,

---

1. Edwin F. Kalmus Music Publishers, P. O. Box 1007, Opa-Locka, Florida 33054.

analyzing, and writing will depend upon the objectives, interests, and abilities of the students.

Courses in composition and modern music are offered at different levels with varying prerequisites. These studies can be undertaken successfully with a minimal background of traditional harmony. Training in counterpoint, orchestration, and form is helpful but not essential.

In addition to doing specific assignments, students should be encouraged to do free creative writing in the style most natural for them at the moment. Compositions should be in forms and for mediums which are familiar and appealing. Even in the specified writing assignments the creative and expressive aspects should be emphasized. The concept should be one of sound rather than of abstract symbols. This manner of thinking is stimulated by writing for a particular instrument or ensemble with complete tempo, phrasing, dynamic, and articulation indications.

Whenever possible written exercises should be played with due regard for interpretation on the instrument(s) for which they are intended. For practical reasons much of the writing will be for piano, which is both versatile and accessible. It is wise in the early stages to avoid extraneous problems and to write for instruments one plays or with which one is familiar, but before the end of the course all available resources, including electronic, should be explored.

Students should see and hear each other's work and participate in discussions. Active participation motivates the class. Analysis of the mistakes and accomplishments of its members is informative and illuminating.

Sketchbooks of thematic ideas and files of creative exercises should be maintained as storehouses of raw material for future works. The muses are elusive and not always at the composer's beck and call.

A public performance of a new work is a stimulating experience for the composer and an illuminating experience for the performers. The full cycle of composition is achieved only when a work has been conceived, written, played, and heard. Through participation in the complete sequence composers become intimately aware of the practical problems of preparing and presenting their scores. This helps them to discover simple and effective ways of notating and developing their ideas. If the performance is recorded, they have the added advantage of repeated, undistracted hearings and opportunities to evaluate their works objectively after the heat of creation has cooled. The value of such experiences cannot be rivaled by abstract instruction.

The reasons for all serious students of music to be informed in the mysteries and mechanics of composition are compelling in this age when performers, and even listeners, are increasingly involved in the realization of musical events and when avant-garde styles are departing so radically from the sounds and symbols of the past. During periods of diversity and change like the present, becoming familiar with all of the trends is difficult but important for the future of the art. One final suggestion—the validity of which is most certain—the only way to learn to compose is by composing.

Introduction

$\mathcal{S}$TUDENTS majoring in music invariably complete a series of courses dealing with the theoretical aspects of traditional music. Logically, studies in contemporary music and composition should follow to update the students' knowledge and to encourage their creativity. Certainly those who have experienced the problems and pleasures of composing bring added insight to their other musical activities, and composing is one of the best ways to develop that intangible but highly significant quality ambiguously called, for want of a more precise term, musicianship. It is accepted as normal for composers to play. Should it not be just as normal for players to compose?

Composition is too often regarded as a mystic art the practice of which is limited to a few great men of genius. A more realistic view is that the potential ability to compose is as widespread as the ability to play an instrument or to sing. Few attain the stature of a Beethoven or a Stravinsky in composition, but how many attain the stature of a Heifetz or a Rubinstein in performance? The answer to this question does not discourage thousands from starting the study of violin and piano every year, and it should not discourage embryonic composers. The urge to compose may come later and be more difficult to express, but it is very likely just as innate and prevalent as the urge to sing and play.

The study of composition has suffered from romantic emphasis on its inspirational elements and neglect of its technical aspects. Young composers are conditioned to think that inspiration cannot be taught or learned and should come therefore as readily to the novice as to the master. Even if this were true, it would not eliminate the necessity for training in composition any more than great talent eliminates the necessity for study and practice in performance.

The fact that everyone begins the study of music as a performer complicates the problem of teaching composition. Prior experience as performer and listener develops the ability to criticize and evaluate far beyond the ability to create. It requires patience on the part of the aspiring composer to develop his creative talents to the point where he is satisfied with his own efforts. During this developmental period, it is reassuring to realize that the works generally known of even the greatest composers come from their mature period and are not representative of their earliest efforts. Activities as a performer and listener are invaluable for the composer, but they do not automatically provide him with compositional skill.

A further complicating factor is the strong emphasis on the music of the romantic period in our musical conditioning. The musical idiom with which we are saturated is ill suited to contemporary ideas. In this regard, the traditional theoretical training provides little direct help. However, if creativity has been encouraged in prior theoretical studies and discipline has been based on general principles rather than on rigid rules of a particular style, the transition can be made with minimal difficulty.

The current practice of basing the early theoretical training of musicians on the music of the eighteenth and nineteenth centuries has the advantages of a vast literature which has stood the test of time and in which the materials and procedures are relatively uniform and comparatively simple. No such advantages exist for new music, but between the old and the new lies a body of twentieth-century music which can be analyzed and described in terms of its relationship to traditional practices. Exploring these relationships helps to bridge the gap between familiar and unfamiliar styles. The course charted on the following pages leads from the post-romantic idioms of the first half of this century to the most recent developments using a typical undergraduate background in tonal music as a point of departure. The suggested assignments for this chapter can be used to assess competence in traditional styles and to reveal any deficiencies that should be remedied by review.

Suggested Assignments

1. Harmonize the following chorale melody in a conventional four-part style observing the traditional principles of chord choice, voice leading, spacing, and doubling.

Ex. 1 VULPIUS: *Chorale*

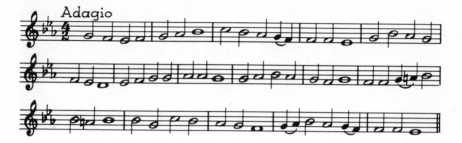

2. Harmonize the following folk song in a free piano style using conventional chords and progressions.

Ex. 2 FOLK SONG: *The Ash Grove*

Melodic Contour
and Organization

OF all the aspects of musical composition, the ability to write effective melodies is the most elusive, the most dependent upon natural gifts, and the most difficult to teach. But if one must rely upon natural gifts for the original conception of a melody, he can employ technique to put it in its most effective form and to make the best use of it.

Some composers seem to have been fortunate enough to conceive perfect melodies spontaneously. Mozart and Schubert apparently had this facility to a remarkable degree, but more often the original concept requires careful revision before it achieves maximum effectiveness. The sketchbooks of Beethoven provide ample proof of both the necessity and the value of such revision.

Example 3 shows various versions of the first eight measures of the second movement theme of Beethoven's *Third Symphony*. The first five versions, with certain alternate measures, appear in Beethoven's sketchbook for 1803 as edited by Nottebohm (Breitkopf and Haertel, 1880). The final version is the theme as it appears in the symphony. Beethoven wrote no key signature in the sketches, but the three flats appear to be intended throughout, corresponding with the final form. A study of these sketches reveals the evolution of a commonplace germ idea, through various stages, into a classic melody. They also reveal how a master craftsman like Beethoven approached the problem of perfecting a crude original melodic thought. The lack of interest in the second phrase of the first version is corrected, and the dotted rhythm which occurs only once in the first version becomes a characteristic unifying factor in the later versions. Every feature of the completed melody appears in the sketches, but none is exactly like it. The finished product is a composite of the best elements arrived at progressively. There is but slight hint of strength and beauty in the original idea, but Beethoven had the technique and preserverance to realize its potential. These abilities are essential to the composer, for it is in this way many of the best melodies are produced.

Ex. 3 BEETHOVEN: *Symphony No. 3 in E-flat* (1804)

Unfortunately, the sketches of composers are not generally available, but much can be learned about their creative process as it affects melodic contour and organization through a study of the melodies in their works. Whether these melodies were created spontaneously or resulted from numerous revisions, they represent the version on which the composer put his final seal of approval. As such they provide models of structural and linear organization, and elements they have in common may well serve as criteria for evaluating and improving melodies of less mature composers.

Analysis is of necessity limited to features which can be observed objectively, though there exists in the best melodies an elusive quality which defies analysis. A penetration of this mystery is not possible or necessary for the composer any more than a full knowledge of life is necessary for a doctor. It suffices for the composer to recognize the strengths and weaknesses of his ideas and to be able to develop the one and eliminate the other.

Characteristics of effective melodic writing can be observed in the following twentieth-century melodies. The principles involved are equally apparent and valid in the music of previous periods, for contemporary practice is a continuation of tradition in matters of melodic contour and organization. Some twentieth-century melodies demonstrate no new technical features, while others are expressed in terms distinctly peculiar to the period. The basic principles can be illustrated most clearly by examples drawn from the former. There is considerable variation in style, design, and length, but each presents a single idea ending with a more or less complete cadence. Single, complete musical ideas can be stated in a variety of ways, all of which are known generally as periods or sentences. Various typical period structures and contours are illustrated in the following examples.

Example 4 uses only the most conventional materials, diatonic notes of E major and equal divisions of the beat. Structurally, it provides a model for one of the most common patterns—one which abounds in folk music and is particularly appropriate for stating songlike melodies. The two halves of the melody begin similarly. The first ends with an incomplete cadence; the second with a complete cadence. The number of measures and the amount of repetition vary in this type of period. The basic elements are the similar beginnings of the two phrases and the incomplete and complete cadence implications. Stepwise motion is predominant in the melody, and scale-line motion in the opposite direction invariably follows the descending fifths. There is a balance between the notes above and below the starting pitch. A climactic effect is lacking, because the highest note comes in both the first and third phrases. The scale line up from C-sharp in the eighth measure provides an effective bridge into the return of the opening. To fully appreciate the importance of this bridge, play the melody substituting a half note (like the other similar places) on C-sharp. Rhythmic motion at this point is essential to preserve the flow of the melody.

Ex. 4 STRAVINSKY: *Firebird Suite* (1910) p18[1]

Example 5 illustrates different features of structure and contour with equally conventional materials. The period consists of two contrasting phrases, a structure as common as that illustrated in Example 4. Interest is added by the extension of the second phrase effected by repeating the material of measure six in measure seven. The low first note introduces a phrase leading to a climax point an octave higher at the semicadence. The climactic effect of this pitch is heightened by its duration and its repetition. Its significance is apparent though the pitch is exceeded by one step before the line begins its downward motion. In this typical contour ascending motion preceding the high point balances the descending motion following it. Two quarter notes on the first beat of the measure followed by descending motion to a note of longer value constitute the characteristic feature of the melody. This device occurs in five of the nine measures. In each instance, besides occurring on different pitches, it is subtly altered to avoid monotony while providing a strong unifying factor. The descending interval is successively a second, a fourth, a third, and finally a fifth. Only the fifth occurs more than once, and this is in connection with the extension. Since the melody is only part of a more extended composition, finality in the cadence is avoided by using the third of the scale instead of the tonic.

---

1. Page numbers refer to the location of the excerpt in the edition indicated, if any; otherwise in the Kalmus score.

Ex. 5 VAUGHAN WILLIAMS: *The Wasps Overture* (1909) p23[1]

The contour of Example 6, which descends to a low point and then reverses direction, is essentially an inversion of that in the preceding example. A telling melodic idea is stated in a concise five-measure phrase. Such short ideas frequently are repeated immediately, as this one is in the complete work. The repeated phrase has period function, and it represents another method of presenting a melodic idea. Unlike the period of Example 4, which it resembles, the cadences are the same for the statement and the repetition. Opportunities for internal repetition in a theme as brief as this are limited, but the two instances of dotted rhythm provide a unifying element, as does the recurrence at the end of the notes A, F-sharp, E from the beginning.

Ex. 6 PROKOFIEV: *Classical Symphony in D* (1917) p55

Of the preceding melodies, the contour of the Vaughan Williams with the high point in the middle is encountered much more frequently than that of the Prokofiev or the Stravinsky, but the most prevalent contour of all is illustrated in Example 7. Here the ascending motion of the first phrase culminates in a secondary high point, but the highest point and real climax is reached near the end of the melody following some preliminary descending motion at the beginning of the second phrase. This basic contour, in which a major portion of the melody is devoted to ascending

8

motion and the climax comes toward the end, is typical of melodies in which the climax constitutes a predominant feature.

Example 7 is another period with contrasting phrases. The one-measure extension of the second phrase is achieved by delaying the resolution of the penultimate note. The treatment of the unifying devices is particularly interesting. The first five beats are repeated immediately, but interest is maintained by the rhythmic shift. Immediate repetition occurs similarly at the beginning of the second phrase. The repetition of this fragment corresponds rhythmically to the statement, but the substitution of eighth notes for quarter notes brings it to a different pitch. The eighth-note neighboring tones of measures one and three are echoed in measure seven in a manner reminiscent of the usage of the dotted figure in Example 6. These neighboring tones also serve to stress the climactic effect of the E-flat in measure eight.

Ex. 7 PROKOFIEV: *Violin Concerto No. 2 in Gm* (1935) p1

Still another contour and organization are illustrated in Example 8. The germ of this melody is contained in the motive which appears sequentially three times. A rapid ascent to the high point near the beginning is followed by a sequential descent to the cadence. This contour is not uncommon, but sequences of this sort are frowned on by many composers. Their excessive use rapidly becomes monotonous and causes stagnation in the melodic flow, but used in moderation and particularly when varied, they provide a strong unifying factor. Though the design of the motive is constant in this example, the quality of the arpeggio, is different in each statement (major, diminished, minor) along with similar changes in the other intervals. Additional interest in melodies containing sequences is generally provided by the harmony and counterpoint associated with them. This melody is only a phrase long, but it sounds perfectly complete in the slow tempo and with its strong cadence. Thematic interest is at a minimum in the last measure, and it serves little purpose other than to bring the phrase to a close.

Ex. 8 RACHMANINOFF: *Symphony No. 2 in Em* (1907) p124

In contrast to the previous example which made use of sequential repetition, the following shows immediate but varied repetition at the same pitch. In each instance the type of alteration is different. The repetition of the first section comes a beat later in the measure, and the end is altered to lead into the next section. The repetition of this section is literal except for the melodic embellishment of the last two beats. The characteristic rest on the beat in the third fragment is strikingly interrupted in the repetition by the accented C-sharp in measure eleven, and the process is reversed in measure twelve where the rest replaces the accent. Each successive motive is shorter than its predecessor, and the repetition is consistently abbreviated or embellished. The internal structure, like that of many of the most interesting melodies, does not conform to any traditional pattern. The high point of the line comes near the middle, and, consistent with the character of the melody, is repeated. The way each motive leads into the next with an overlapping which makes it impossible to determine exactly where one ends and the other begins must be ranked as a stroke of genius.

Ex. 9 RAVEL: *Piano Sonatine* (1905) p2

Though a large percentage of melodies are cast in periods made up of two phrases, any number of phrases may be used, and periods of three and four phrases are common. Any presentation of a single, complete musical idea, regardless of the number of phrases it contains, is functionally a period.

Example 10, which is a rather unusual group of five phrases and quite unlike the previous examples in structure, illustrates the flexibility possible in phrase organization. It is unlike the previous examples in still another way. Though it is the longest melody examined thus far, it exploits the most meager resources. Few composers choose to limit themselves to such drastic economy of means. In the entire twenty measures only two rhythmic patterns occur within a measure, and four of the five phrases are identical in rhythm and similar in shape. When such economy is practiced, even the slightest variation assumes exaggerated importance, and Sibelius is careful to provide a token change in each phrase. Phrase three duplicates phrase one a third higher with resultant changes in the quality of the intervals. Phrase four stands in the same relation to phrase two. The most notable deviation from the pattern and the one which does the most to rescue this melody from monotony, however, is the shift of the characteristic grace notes and dotted rhythm from the third measure of the phrase to the first in the concluding phrase, which ends with an implied but unsounded cadence. Unusual economy of means and irregular phrase structure are coupled with the most ordinary contour. The high point of the melody comes toward the end, associated with the only dynamic change.

Ex. 10 SIBELIUS: *Pelleas and Melisande* (1905) p5

For sheer number of notes involved, the theme of Ravel's *Bolero* must certainly rank as one of the most extensive melodies. For this reason it presents a particularly interesting example of musical organization. Divided in the middle by a comparatively strong semicadence, each half descends through a series of figures to the low C. The position of the high point in the middle is usual enough, but the approach to it is unique. It comes at the beginning of a phrase after a rest and is approached by leap instead of by the more usual gradual ascending motion. Though the rythmic subtlety of this melody can be appreciated fully only in association with its accompaniment, the skillful exploitation of rhythm is apparent, even isolated. The first impression is one of remarkable unity, but closer examination reveals a great diversity of detail. The only device which consistently recurs is that of the tie into the beat. This device appears twelve times, but even here the element of diversity is present. These twelve ties join **seven** different rhythmic combinations. Such ingenius manipulation of materials is evidence of technical skill.

Ex. 11 RAVEL: *Bolero* (1927) p2

No discussion of melodic writing, even in the twentieth century, is complete without some mention of those emotion-packed melodies typical of the romantic era. For many people this type of melody is almost synonymous with the word. Though no longer in vogue with the majority of composers, the ability to write such a tune is a priceless gift in any age. The difficulty of drawing with certainty the fine line between emotion and sentiment is perhaps one reason this aspect of the art is neglected now. The following example has become somewhat hackneyed through popular adaptions, but in the original it represents highly emotional writing at its finest. With this type of melody particularly, analysis of its external characteristics provides minimal insight. Its appeal is essentially subjective. The cadence points though somewhat camouflaged can be located, and the phrases though unclearly delineated can be isolated. The climax point is effectively prepared and strategically located. The lowered sixth degree of the scale, G-flat in the key of B-flat, imparts a distinctive flavor to the melody. The sum of these features fails to account for the total effect. It stems rather from some impelling logic which defies analysis but which makes each note when heard in context sound inevitable. In a melody this is a paramount virtue.

Ex. 12 RACHMANINOFF: *Piano Concerto No. 2 in Cm* (1901) p78

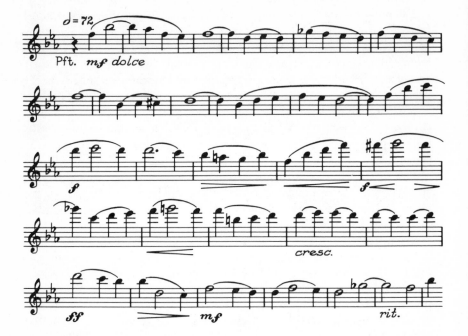

The foregoing examples provide a basis for some observations regarding desirable melodic characteristics. Perhaps no tune possesses all of them, and excellent melodies have contrary features. This does not detract from the essential validity of principles based on the normal practices of recognized composers. There is no formula for writing good melodies, but these models and suggestions will prove helpful in locating and correcting weaknesses, in evaluating results, and in putting creative efforts in their most effective form. The existence of completely conventional melodies in twentieth-century music demonstrates that the older resources remain viable in the evolutionary process while the newer ones are being explored.

Melodic ideas vary greatly in length. The idea itself determines what is appropriate. Longer melodies divide into phrases delineated by cadences. The location and distribution of these cadences are extremely important. The cadence at the conclusion of an idea does not present a serious problem in melodies of definite tonality. They end on a note of the tonic chord—root for the most conclusive, third of fifth for less conclusive closes. The cadential function must be clear, but trite formulas should be

14

avoided. In cadences other than at the end of a work or movement the beginning of the next phrase should not be delayed too long, but the duration of the cadence note is not critical.

Incomplete cadences within a melody serve to pace the exposition of melodic ideas with a flow that is neither choppy nor aimless. The former results from cadence points too close together and too strong; the latter from cadence points too far apart and too weak. Semicadences most often are accomplished by momentary interruptions in the rhythmic flow. The proper duration for these interruptions is a subjective matter, but they should provide breathing places without causing loss of interest. Semicadences may occur on any pitch, and no one note should be overworked. Care should be exercised not to anticipate the finality of the complete cadence.

The statement of a musical idea can be entirely in one key like the examples, or it can modulate. A transient modulation can be followed by a return to the original key for the complete cadence, or another key can be established by a sufficiently strong cadence in the new key.

Repetition is evident in most melodies. Coupled with a charactistic feature, which it often is, repetition provides a powerful unifying factor. For interest, repetitions are varied and embellished. Common types of modification include changes in intervals, pitch location, key, mode, rhythm, dynamics, and combinations of these.

A characteristic feature distinguishes most good melodies. No melody is unique in every detail, but some element must set it apart. The notable feature may be a rhythm, an interval, a motive, or anything which will serve as a means of identification.

In rhythm there should be balance between unity and variety. Notes of equal value and constant patterns lack rhythmic interest. Perpetual changes of duration and pattern reduce coherence. A limited number of patterns and values used with imagination is most effective.

Stepwise motion is basic in melodic writing, to which is added the spice of varied skips. Skips except along chord line are generally followed by a change of direction, often by step.

Melodic units with but one thought usually have a single focal point. This focal point, or climax, is most frequently associated with the highest pitch. The climactic effect can be enhanced by rhythmic prolongation, embellishments, and dynamics. A typical melodic line is concerned with approaching and leaving the focal point in the most effective manner. There is no formula for this, but it is of primary importance. The graphs of Examples 4 through 12, given in Example 13, show some typical melodic contours. The main climax usually is approached or followed by a series of lesser high points. A balance between ascending and descending motion is desirable, but the distribution must be determined subjectively. Too much emphasis on any one pitch is monotonous. This is especially true when the recurring note comes at cadences and at high, low, and turning points in the melody.

Ex. 13. CONTOUR GRAPHS OF EXAMPLES 4 THROUGH 12

(a) Graph of Example 4

E

(b) Graph of Example 5

E♭

(c) Graph of Example 6

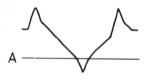

A

(d) Graph of Example 7

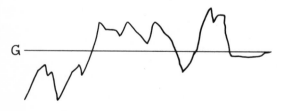

G

(e) Graph of Example 8

A

(f) Graph of Example 9 (octave embellishments omitted)

F♯

(g) Graph of Example 10

F

F

(h) Graph of Example 11

C

(i) Graph of Example 12

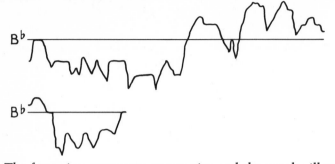

The foregoing comments summarize and the graphs illustrate characteristics of the examples and, indeed, of good melodies generally. It is admittedly easier to list the characteristics than to create melodies which embody them, because the quality of a melody is more dependent upon balance than upon the possession of specific features. Balance is essential between unity and variety, activity and repose, ascending and descending motion, conjunct and disjunct motion, cadences, and climaxes, but the perception of balance is subjective. Subjective judgments to have validity must be based on a foundation of thorough knowledge and broad experience. Instincts sharpened by analyzing and conceiving conventional melodies are readily adapted to evaluating and composing themes using expanded tonal resources and in more progressive idioms.

Suggested Assignments

1. Analyze the melodic contour and internal organization of the themes from Prokofiev's *Classical Symphony.*
2. Examine early twentieth-century scores to find conventional melodies illustrating various contours. List the scores examined by composer and title. Copy the melodies and write brief analyses of their salient features.
3. Write original melodies in a traditional style, at first deliberately imitating the models. Later, concentrate on developing strength of thematic idea and effectiveness of presentation in a more personal manner.
4. Make contour graphs of the melodies written for Assignment 3 and check them for compliance with the principles outlined in this chapter. Revise the melodies as necessary to eliminate any flaws that are detected.
5. Read the chapters on melody in *The Shaping Forces in Music* by Ernst Toch (Wehman reprint).

3

Modal Melodic Resources

CONTEMPORARY musicians have not been concerned exclusively with blazing unexplored trails. They have also done extensive research on early music, much of which is based on a system of modal scales. It is not the historic uses of the modes that interest composers but rather their effectiveness in counteracting restrictive major-minor conditioning. The modal scales, neglected by composers for three centuries, provide a simple and logical extension of melodic resources.

Ignoring historical implications, the modal scales consist of seven tones with a different pattern of five whole steps and two half steps for each mode. All of the modes are produced by playing seven-tone scales on the white keys of the piano starting on successive notes. The names, of Greek origin, are given in Example 14, and the locations of the semitones are marked for ready comparison. The major and natural minor scales form part of the modal system as the Ionian and Aeolian modes. The other modes are like one or the other of these with one scale degree altered, except Locrian which has two. Notes which differ from major or minor are indicated by arrows pointing in the direction of the deviation.

Ex. 14 THE MODES

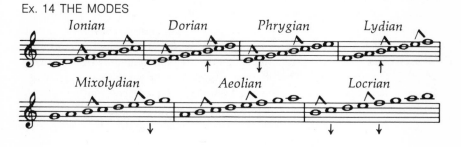

The arrangement of the whole steps and half steps in the modes is in every way just as natural as in major and minor, and the use of a mode as a source of material for a melody is just as valid. The modes are not to be considered as altered major or minor scales. However, ears saturated with major and minor music are apt to perceive them in terms of their deviation from the major-minor patterns, and this deviation then asserts itself as the distinctive feature of the mode. In preliminary work with the modes it is useful to keep this feature in mind and to exploit it consciously. The following table showing the deviation of each mode from major or natural minor is given for reference.

Ionian . . . . . . like major
Dorian . . . . . . like minor with the sixth degree raised
Phrygian . . . . like minor with the second degree lowered
Lydian . . . . . . like major with the fourth degree raised
Mixolydian . . . like major with the seventh degree lowered
Aeolian . . . . . like minor
Locrian . . . . . like minor with the second and fifth degrees lowered

It is emphasized that the modes were not derived from the major and minor scales, but students trained in traditional harmony usually find this association and the association of the untransposed modes with the white keys of the piano the easiest ways to recognize and remember them.

A distinction must be maintained between the characteristic notes of the modes and the occurrence of these same relationships as chromatic tones in tonal (i. e., major or minor) melodies. As chromatic notes they have an auxiliary function and a decided tendency to resolve in the direction of the alteration. By contrast, their function in the modes is basic, and they are free to progress either up or down by step or skip. They behave exactly like diatonic notes which, in the modes, they actually are.

The modes can be transposed to any pitch in the same manner as major and minor by using accidentals or the proper signature to produce the required pattern of whole steps and half steps. A formula for modal signatures can be derived from the relationship of the untransposed mode to C major. For example, the Dorian mode is like a major scale beginning on its second degree, or stated another way, the Dorian mode has the same signature as the major scale a major second below. Thus, the Dorian mode on G would have the same signature as the major scale a tone below, which is F with one flat. The Phrygian mode has the same signature as the major scale a major third below, so Phrygian on C-sharp would have the same signature as A major or three sharps. This process can be continued to determine the signature for any mode on any pitch. The fact that a mode has the same signature as some major scale must not be construed to constitute a relationship between them.

Essentially this same process will serve to determine the mode when the tonic and the signature are known. For example, if the tonic (the *final* in modal terminology) is A and the signature is four sharps, the mode would be Lydian since the signature is that of the major scale a perfect fourth below.

There is no uniform practice in the use of signatures for modal music. Some composers use the signature which produces the mode without the use of accidentals. Others use the major or minor signature which is closest to that of the mode and then add the necessary accidentals. This practice is usual when only part of the composition is modal. In many recent works there are no signatures, and accidentals are used as required. This practice has the same advantages and disadvantages in modal as in tonal writing. When there are frequent shifts in the key center, it avoids the problem of excessive cancellations, but sharps and flats must be indicated each time they occur.

The following melodies from the works of twentieth-century composers are written in a mode or show evidence of modal influence, though it is possible that the influence functioned on a subconscious level with no deliberate intent on the composer's part to utilize modal elements. The perception of tonal centers is somewhat subjective, so there are times when the tonal center and consequently the mode are open to more than one interpretation. In some cases, too, the accompanying parts suggest a center different from that of the melody. These facts, however, do not detract from the genuine contribution of modal concepts to the music of this century.

The F-sharp does not appear in the signature of Example 15, but it is used consistently. The cadences are on C and A alternately. The scale on C with F-sharp is Lydian, but Dorian on A emerges as the mode of this example and the movement from which it is taken.

Ex. 15 BARTOK: *Piano Sonatina* (1915) p5

A more extended melody in D Dorian is given in Example 16. G-sharp occurs five times as a chromatic neighboring tone, but in each instance it resolves as such without disrupting the feeling for the mode. In contrast, the B-natural which is diatonic in the mode, though raised from the signature, more often than not resolves downward. The B-flat near the end of the melody suggests a change to the Aeolian mode, and the final E-flat results in a modulation.

Ex. 16 SIBELIUS: *Violin Concerto in Dm* (1903) p3

The Phrygian mode with its center on G is illustrated in Example 17.

Ex. 17 VAUGHAN WILLIAMS: *Fantasia on a Theme by Tallis* (1910) p23

The setting for Example 18 suggests D minor, but the melody considered by itself is a particularly clear and beautiful example of Phrygian on A.

22

Ex. 18 RAVEL: *String Quartet in F* (1903) p5

International Music Company

The distinction between major and Lydian is not always clear because of the frequent use of the raised fourth degree of the scale in major. Also, the use of the augmented fourth above the tonic, the characteristic note of the Lydian mode, tends to create the impression of a modulation to the dominant. Example 19 is an unambiguous Lydian melody on C, though for the first three measures the other parts imply Dorian on A. Writing a melody that suggests one mode and an accompaniment that suggests another seems to have been a device Ravel favored.

Ex. 19 RAVEL: *String Quartet in F* (1903) p30

International Music Company

F-sharp as a chromatic tone in C major has a denfinite tendency to resolve upward. Since the descending motion continues after the F-sharp in Example 20, the Lydian influence is apparent even though the next fragment suggests C major.

Ex. 20 HANSON: *Symphony No. 2 "Romantic"* (1930) p32

The feature of the major scale which composers find most restricting is the tendency of the leading tone to resolve up to the tonic. This tendency is so strong that in many progressions no other voice leading is satisfactory. For this reason melodic lines and harmonic progressions involving the leading tone have been most subject to stereotyping. Finding an effective substitute for the clichés involving the leading tone is one of the most perplexing problems for composers breaking away from traditional formulas. One solution is to avoid the leading tone, and this is provided by the Mixolydian mode, which otherwise has all the characteristics of major. This accounts for the frequency with which Mixolydian is used and perhaps for the excellence of extended melodies conceived entirely in it. The next three examples are representative.

In spite of the key signature the mode of Example 21 is Mixolydian on D. The mode is pure except for the C-sharp in the thirty-second note run leading to the octave transposition in the second phrase.

Ex. 21 VAUGHAN WILLIAMS: *The Wasps Overture* (1909) p8

In Britten's *Serenade for Tenor, Horn, and Strings* the *Prologue,* which is repeated as the *Epilogue,* is for unaccompanied French horn. It is played without using the valves, so the pitches deviate perceptibly from equal temperament. The complete notation is given in Example 22. It is in the Mixolydian mode on F throughout.

Ex. 22 BRITTEN: *Serenade—Prologue* (1943)

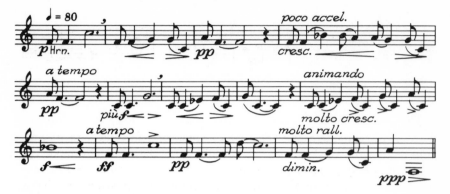

Example 23 is another extended melody in pure Mixolydian, this one untransposed on G.

Ex. 23 COPLAND: *Violin Sonata* (1943) p17

Because the melodic and harmonic forms of minor are used almost exclusively in traditional music, the natural minor or Aeolian has a relatively fresh sound even though it is studied along with major in common practice theory. Example 24, which is pure Aeolian on D, exhibits the special qualities of this mode in a line that would be impossibly distorted by the chromatic adjustments of melodic or harmonic minor.

Ex. 24 SHOSTAKOVICH: *Symphony No. 5* (1937) p109

The Locrian mode is rarely encountered in the music of any period. Some theorists recognize it in theory only and argue that it has no practical applications. Example 25 would appear to be an exception. Only one chromatic passing tone in the melody is not in the Locrian mode on B, and all of the notes of the scale are used except A. The missing A, however, is prominent in the accompaniment and seems to assert itself as the tonal center, making the mode Aeolian. The F-sharps that appear in four measures of the accompaniment can be attributed to Dorian influence. The notes of the cadence chord, B–D–F–A, suggest the Locrian mode, but the A is in the bass and it sounds like the tonal center. It is the possibility of multiple interpretations such as this that accounts for part of the subtle charm of modal melodies.

Ex. 25 KHACHATURIAN: *Violin Concerto* (1940) p24

Academic distinctions are sometimes made between Ionian and major, but for purposes of composition and analysis they are identical. Since all of the major melodies in Chapter 2 can also be regarded as Ionian, no examples of Ionian are included here. Additional examples of melodies in the other modes can be found in the section on modal quality in Chapter 7.

The characteristic structure of each modal scale is responsible in part for the effectiveness of melodies based on it. This fact can be demonstrated impressively by playing the foregoing examples substituting notes of the parallel major or minor scales for the distinctive notes of the modes. By such seemingly trivial corruptions some of the most impressive melodies can become commonplace, which is further evidence that regarding the modes as merely variants of more familiar scales is fallacious.

The modes put at the composer's disposal not only a variety of scale resources, but collectively they make all twelve pitches accessible without chromatic implications, as is demonstrated in Example 26 showing all of the modes starting on C.

Ex. 26 THE MODES STARTING ON C

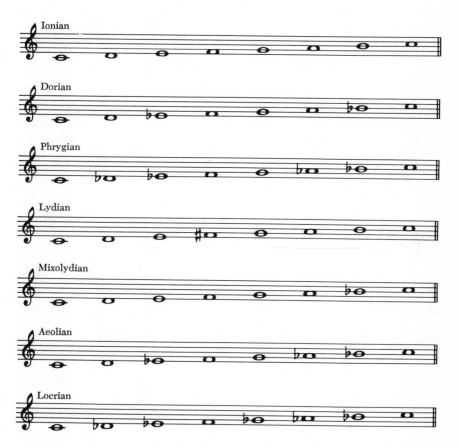

Example 27 is a composite of the notes in Example 26 listing the modes in which each note occurs.

Ex. 27 COMPOSITE OF THE MODES STARTING ON C

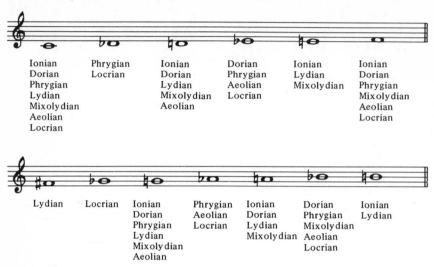

Ionian	Phrygian	Ionian	Dorian	Ionian	Ionian
Dorian	Locrian	Dorian	Phrygian	Lydian	Dorian
Phrygian		Lydian	Aeolian	Mixolydian	Phrygian
Lydian		Mixolydian	Locrian		Mixolydian
Mixolydian		Aeolian			Aeolian
Aeolian					Locrian
Locrian					

Lydian	Locrian	Ionian	Phrygian	Ionian	Dorian	Ionian
		Dorian	Aeolian	Dorian	Phrygian	Lydian
		Phrygian	Locrian	Lydian	Mixolydian	
		Lydian		Mixolydian	Aeolian	
		Mixolydian			Locrian	
		Aeolian				

Since the modes have much in common with major and minor and are a definite part of our musical heritage, they offer an ideal approach to expanding melodic resources beyond the arbitrary limitations of major and minor.

Suggested Assignments

1. Write the proper signature for the following modes:
   a. Dorian on E
   b. Aeolian on F
   c. Lydian on B-flat
2. Name the mode when:
   a. The signature is two sharps and the tonal center is A
   b. The signature is four flats and the tonal center is C
   c. The signature is one sharp and the tonal center is F-sharp
3. Determine the tonal center and mode of the themes in Ravel's *String Quartet in F*. Observe the changes in recurrences of the themes.
4. Locate additional twentieth-century melodies which exhibit modal influences.
5. Write original melodies in each of the modes. At first use pure modes with a definite tonal center and exploit their characteristic features. Later apply modal concepts freely in spontaneous melodic invention.

Twentieth Century
Melodic Practices

THE free transposition of either the major-minor or modal scales requires all twelve of the notes accommodated by conventional notation and playable on standard instruments. The twelve tones in an octave became practical when the principle of equal temperament was widely adopted more than two hundred years ago, but new ways of exploiting them are still being found.

Prior to 1900 the prevailing practice was to derive melodic materials from the seven tones of a definite key or mode and to use the remaining five notes incidentally for embellishment and variety. Modern practice is to utilize more fully the potential of the available pitches through greater freedom in linear organization, more varied scale resources, less restrictive concepts of tonality, and by responding to contemporary harmonic influences. These trends are examined in this chapter and illustrated with melodies from the literature. The features which distinguish twentieth-century melodic writing are not clearly delineated and used independently, but for purposes of study it simplifies the problem to consider them individually.

Nonvocal Melodic Lines

Vocal influences permeate the melodies of the classic and romantic periods, even in instrumental works. Singable melodies are the norm for these periods, and singableness is still cited on occasion as a factor in melodic value. This test is less applicable to the music of the baroque era and has very little validity for the music of the present. While many melodies can be sung with ease, other equally good melodies are decidedly nonvocal and unsingable.

One of the ways nonvocal characteristics are manifest is in the use of extended ranges. In view of the wide ranges practical on orchestral and keyboard instruments, it is remarkable that so many melodies written for them observe the limitations of the voice. The next three examples are among those that do not. The essential lyric quality of the violin and of many vocal melodies is preserved in Example 28 while covering a range in excess of two octaves within three measures.

Ex. 28 PROKOFIEV: *Violin Concerto No. 2 in Gm* (1935) p3

The Example 29 melody ranges over the keyboard with wide leaps and octave transpositions without which its effect would be greatly diminished, as can be demonstrated by transposing the first two measures up an octave and the last two measures down an octave.

Ex. 29 COPLAND: *Piano Sonata* (1941) p3

From the same work as the preceding example, Example 30 shows another procedure leading to extended melodic ranges. Here the extended range is the result of leaps which continue in the same direction instead of reversing in the traditional manner.

30

Ex. 30 COPLAND: *Piano Sonata* (1941) p19

Leaps of more than an octave within a phrase are intrinsically nonvocal in style. Such leaps sometimes result from what appear to be octave transpositions of melodic fragments even though there are no repetitions at the octave. Example 31 is a melody of this type: (a) as Milhaud wrote it and (b) with fragments transposed an octave and wide leaps reduced correspondingly.

Ex. 31 MILHAUD: *Violin Concerto No. 2* (1948) p8

(a)

(b)

It is not to be presumed that composers conceive melodies with conventional contours and then transpose segments of them, but this type of analysis reveals affinities between some angular twentieth-century melodies and their smoother counterparts which otherwise might not be apparent. When the melodic segments in different octaves consist of only one or two notes as in Example 32, the angularity is extreme. The characteristic ninth interval, which results from an octave expansion of a second, occurs four times and is the interval spanned by the arpeggios in measures two and four.

Ex. 32 PROKOFIEV: *Symphony No. 5* (1944) p61

The ultimate in octave expansion of intervals is illustrated in Example 33 where alternate notes are in different octaves. The consistent alternation of registers could lead to the perception of two melodic streams, one in the upper octave and the other in the lower, but this effect is minimized by the short duration of the low notes. Transposed up an octave, they would be simple chromatic neighboring tones.

Ex. 33 SCHOENBERG: *Three Piano Pieces, Op. 11 No. 1* (1910) p4

Some melodies for voice are as unvocal in style as those for instruments. The Example 34 melody for soprano has wide and unusual intervals and an angular contour encompassing more than two octaves. It demands vocal capabilities that were considered impossible until a few decades ago and illustrates how the concept of vocal melody has changed in recent times. However, to sing such a complex melody accurately taxes the most competent professionals, a fact worth remembering when composing for less proficient singers.

32

Ex. 34 BERG: *Wozzeck—Act II Scene 1* (1921) p87

Additional Scale Resources

The scales considered thus far have been limited to those consisting of seven notes comprising five tones and two semitones. Though these scale patterns dominated European music for several centuries, there is no justification for restricting melodic resources to them exclusively. Other scale patterns have always been favored by non-European cultures, and for some time now the trend in Western music has been to borrow scale resources from other musical traditions and to invent new ones. Tracing the origins and geographic distribution of the various scales is a fascinating study, but the primary concern of composers and performers is their utilization in living music.

Pentatonic (five-tone) scales are among the most ancient and universal. The most prevalent pentatonic scale has a pattern like a major scale with the third and seventh degrees omitted or like the black keys of the piano. Example 35 is a Debussy melody containing only sharp notes which can be played on the black piano keys.

Ex. 35 DEBUSSY: *Nocturnes—Nuages* (1899) p12

Any note in a pentatonic scale can serve as the center or tonic, and notes which are stressed or on which cadences occur tend to be heard as such. However, persons accustomed to the strong functional relationships in major and minor never have a comparable sense of tonality in pentatonic music due mainly to its lack of a leading tone. The scale of the preceding example is represented like C-sharp major with the E-sharp and B-sharp omitted, but the tonal center seems to shift from F-sharp at the beginning to G-sharp at the end. A change of center with the same collection of pitches means that there is a corresponding change in the scale pattern, that is, in the arrangement of the major seconds and minor thirds comprising the scale. The next two examples illustrate other pentatonic scale patterns, the first centering on D.

Ex. 36 RAVEL: *String Quartet in F* (1903) p37

International Music Company

In the continuation of the preceding melody, B-flat is introduced in the next measure. Twelve measures later B-flat replaces A in the scale of the following pentatonic melody, which otherwise has the same pitch content. This melody revolves around C but cadences on B-flat. It is a cyclic return of a theme originally stated in the Phrygian mode (see Example 18).

Ex. 37 RAVEL: *String Quartet in F* (1903) p38

Another pentatonic scale prevalent in Japanese music and frequently used to evoke an oriental atmosphere is produced by omitting the third and seventh degrees of a Phrygian scale. The same interval relationships are produced by omitting the second and fifth or sixth degrees of a major scale. Any number of five-tone scales can be devised simply by omitting different notes from the various seven-tone scales. In our musical tradition such scales are not used for extended passages, but Stravinsky often wrote fragmentary melodies using a limited number of notes. The five used in the following melody occur in both the Dorian and Aeolian modes on G.

Ex. 38 STRAVINSKY: *The Rite of Spring* (1913) p17

Example 39 shows a pronounced Phrygian influence, but with the fourth degree missing the remaining notes form identical three-note patterns separated by a major third.

Ex. 39 DEBUSSY: *String Quartet* (1893) p3

A six-tone scale more often associated with Debussy is the whole-tone scale. Whole-tone scales a semitone apart consist of mutually exclusive pitch collections, and one or the other of these collections will duplicate the notes of the whole-tone scale starting on any pitch. Since the potential of whole-tone scales is extremely limited both melodically and harmonically, they are more useful for isolated coloristic passages than as a basis for complete compositions. The source of Example 40 is exceptional. All of its pitches in all but six measures, which are black-key pentatonic, are derived from the whole-tone scale shown. Observe the enharmonic spellings.

Ex. 40 DEBUSSY: *Piano Preludes, Book I No. 2—Voiles* (1910)

Ordinarily the equal intervals and the absence of a leading tone cause the feeling for tonality to be vague or nonexistent in whole-tone music, but Example 41 shows an incidental whole-tone influence in a strongly tonal work. F is the tonic throughout the melody, and the second phrase is in F major. The whole tones seem to have been derived from the first three notes of the ascending F major scale and the first three notes of the

36

descending F minor scale. This results in the mirroring of the two whole steps above F by two whole steps below.

Ex. 41 VAUGHAN WILLIAMS: *The Wasps Overture* (1909) p4

Mirroring of scale degrees is carried further in Example 42 by Bartok. In the most conventional terms, the scale on which it is based is made up of the lower tetrachord of a major scale and the upper tetrachord of a natural or descending melodic minor scale. The scale material also may be analyzed as a mirroring of the first five notes of the major scale, with a tone-tone-semitone pattern both up and down from E. This analysis is supported by the mirror imitation between the two hands.

Ex. 42 BARTOK: *Mikrokosmos, No. 29—Imitation Reflected* (1926–37)

Whatever the derivation of the preceding scale, it affords note combinations not available in major, minor, or any mode. Infinite variety is possible in constructing scales of this sort. For lack of a better and generally accepted designation, such scales will be called *synthetic scales*. Bartok was ingenious in the derivation and use of synthetic scales. Some of his unconventional scale materials seem to have been purely contrived, while others stem from non-Western musical traditions. Synthetic scale structures underlie several pieces in his *Mikrokosmos*. Because of their simplicity they provide an excellent introduction to the device.

In Example 43 unconventional key signatures, different in each hand, produce a synthetic scale. In the piece only those notes shown on the top staff and their octaves are played by the right hand, and only those notes shown on the bottom staff and their octaves are played by the left hand. C is the tonal center. The mirroring of intervals is apparent with the scale notes arranged on the staff as they are in the example and as they occur in the piece. The mirroring, unlike that in the two preceding examples, starts on different notes.

Ex. 43 BARTOK: *Mikrokosmos, No. 99—Crossed Hands* (1926–37)

The key signature of *Mikrokosmos No. 41* is one sharp on C, and its tonal center is G. The scale on which it is based combines features of two modes—the augmented fourth of Lydian with the minor seventh of Mixolydian.

Ex. 44 BARTOK: *Mikrokosmos, No. 41—Melody with Accompaniment* (1926-37)

No signature is used in the source of Example 45. The scale is made up of two major pentachords a tritone apart. The compass extends beyond an octave, which is possible in synthetic scales when different inflections of notes are used in the second octave. It is also possible to use different inflections of a note in the same octave, like the C-natural and the C-sharp. Since each pentachord appears in a different hand, this piece could be perceived as being in two keys simultaneously. Consideration of this possibility is postponed until Chapter 8.

Ex. 45 BARTOK: *Mikrokosmos, No. 86—Two Major Pentachords* (1926–37)

Example 46 shows another synthetic scale resulting from the combination of two key signatures. The signatures themselves are not as unconventional as they appear to be. The E-flat and A-flat which normally precede D-flat in the signature could as well be added to the top part, but they would be meaningless since those notes do not occur in the piece. One sharp on F is not an unusual signature, but it appears unusual when it is placed in the first space. Bartok places the sharp where it occurs in the melody rather than on the fifth line, but the effect is the same. E is the tonal center of the piece. It begins on E and ends on the tritone E, B-flat. The scale consists of alternating whole and half steps up from the tonic. Placing the D-natural below the keynote of the scale, where it occurs in the second violin part, produces an eight-tone scale from D-natural to D-flat with the second note as the keynote. The practice of starting a scale on a note other than the keynote has historical precedent in the plagal forms of the modes.

Ex. 46 BARTOK: *44 Violin Duets, No. 11—Cradle Song* (1931)

Unconventional and double key signatures are useful in devising and notating new scale resources, but they are a hazard for performers who must resist years of conditioning when they encounter a new arrangement of sharps or flats in a signature. They are not too disturbing in scores, but it is generally inadvisable to use them in performance parts, especially when rehearsal time is limited. Preferable procedures are to use no key signature or to use the conventional signature that most closely approximates the synthetic scale and to add accidentals and cancellations as required. The end result is the same, and maximum efficiency in learning the work and performing it accurately are assured.

The recommended procedure is illustrated in Benjamin Britten's *Dirge*, which is based on a synthetic scale. The tonal center is G, and the key signature is that of G minor. A-flat is used consistently, and it could be added to the signature without violating the normal order or arrangement of the flats. However, Britten chooses to indicate it each time with an accidental. The C-sharp in the melody is a chromatic neighboring tone and the D-flat a chromatic changing tone. Omitting them, the scale is like harmonic minor with a lowered second degree or like the Phrygian mode with a raised seventh degree.

Ex. 47 BRITTEN: *Serenade—Dirge* (1943) p18

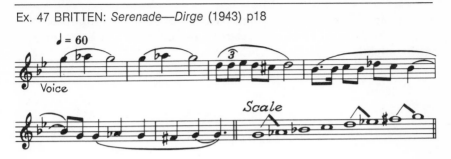

In the source of Example 48 Griffes follows the same procedure as Britten, using the signature of B minor for a melody with B as its tonal center. The scale, with its two augmented seconds, is synthetic as far as the major-minor and modal systems are concerned, but it occurs with sufficient frequency to have a common designation—that of *gypsy scale*. Though not included in our basic scale systems, it is used extensively in other parts of the world. It effectively invokes the oriental atmosphere of the Coleridge poem which inspired the music.

Ex. 48 GRIFFES: *The Pleasure Dome of Kubla Khan* (1919) p16

An eight-tone scale in which half steps and whole steps alternate figures prominently in the music of Stravinsky (see Arthur Berger, "Problems of Pitch Organization in Stravinsky," *Perspectives of New Music* 2/1, 1963). This *octatonic* scale, to use Berger's terminology, is produced by combining the pitches of any two diminished seventh chords, as shown. Since the scale contains four identical three-note patterns, different pitches can be perceived as the tonal center, but only three transpositions are possible. An octatonic scale starting on any note will duplicate the pitch content of one of the scales shown in Example 49.

Ex. 49 OCTATONIC SCALES

The octatonic scale has many fascinating possibilities for both melodic and harmonic constructions. The theme for the variations in Stravinsky's *Octet* is derived from the octatonic scale on A.

Ex. 50 STRAVINSKY: *Octet* (1923) p12

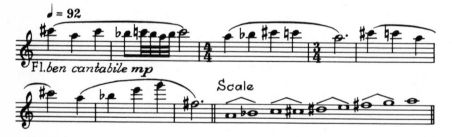

In *The Technique of My Musical Language* Olivier Messiaen describes and illustrates his "theory of the modes of limited transpositions," which includes the octatonic scale as mode 2. Messiaen's modes are not to be confused with any other uses of the term. His modes, derived from the twelve pitches of the tempered system, are formed by combining two or more symmetrical groups with the last note of each group coinciding with the first note of the next. The construction of the modes is such that after a limited number of transpositions—two to six—any further transposition produces a duplicate pitch content. The first mode is identical with the whole-tone scale, for which two transpositions are possible. Three transpositions of the second mode, like the octatonic scale, are possible before the pitch content is repeated. Beginning this mode on its second degree reverses the order of the whole steps and half steps but does not alter the pitch content. The remaining modes of limited transposition are shown starting on C, which Messiaen designates as the first transposition. There are four transpositions of mode 3 and six transpositions of modes 4–7.

Ex. 51 MESSIAEN: *Modes of Limited Transpositions*

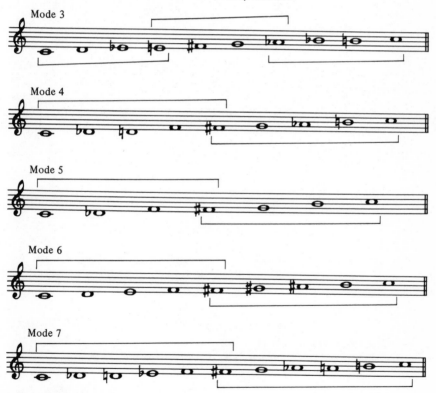

The pitches of mode 3 in its first transposition are used exclusively in the following melody for violin, and in its piano accompaniment in the complete version.

Ex. 52 MESSIAEN: *Theme and Variations* (1932)

Extract from *Theme and Variations* by Olivier Messiaen. Copyright by Alphonse Leduc & Cie, Paris, Owners and Publishers.

This consideration of additional scale resources is by no means exhaustive. It merely indicates some of the new scales that have been used, hints at the manner in which they may have been conceived, and points the way for the creation of additional scale patterns. This technique is valuable, because music based on a selective scale, even a synthetic one, is generally more homogeneous and comprehensible than music lacking such a foundation.

Expanded Tonality

Restrictions resulting from selective scale concepts have diminished continuously during the course of Western music history. By the end of the romantic era chromatic tones were employed to such an extent they rivaled the tones of the scale in importance and frequency of use, though selective scales and tonality had not yet been abandoned. Increased chromaticism coupled with free and frequent modulation led to a greatly expanded concept of tonality. Carried to its logical conclusion, chromaticism leads to an all-inclusive scale of twelve tones with equal status known as a *duodecuple* scale. This designation is more appropriate than chromatic scale even though the notes are the same, because it does not carry with it connotations of altered or secondary tones. The duodecuple scale provides maximum freedom in melodic invention, but the unifying force of selective scales and tonality are lost in the bargain. This poses a problem that has been attacked by contemporary composers in three basic ways.

The first way is simply to deny the importance of tonality—to renounce it as a desirable quality. Music with no tonal center is called *atonal*. Composers of atonal music enjoy the advantages of unlimited freedom, but uninitiated listeners find it difficult to comprehend and appreciate.

The tendency to perceive as a tonic any tone which appears at strategic points such as cadences or is used more frequently than the others is innate or at least strongly conditioned. Therefore, atonality does not occur spontaneously but must be cultivated, and free (i.e., nonserial) atonality is relatively rare. When tonality and selective scale foundations are missing, conceiving infectious melodies is more difficult, but the point at which tonality ceases to function is largely subjective. Some musicians will detect a tonal center in almost any combination of pitches, while others perceive tonality only when definite tonal relationships are established. The former would find evidence to suggest a tonal center, perhaps F, in Example 34, but the latter would probably regard it as atonal.

Example 53 approaches atonality, but it is basically simple. This sort of melody, though lacking strong tonal orientation, has no insurmountable obstacles to comprehension. The triads outlined in the melodic contour provide a link with tradition and previous experience.

Ex. 53 BERG: *Wozzeck—Act I Scene 3* (1914–21) p45

Though free atonality is possible, atonal music more often is based on a *note series* or *tone row* which provides both a systematic way of achieving atonality and a unifying device to take the place of tonality. *Twelve-tone* or *serial* music, as music based on a series or row is called, represents the second twentieth-century approach to musical organization. This approach is considered separately in Chapter 14.

The third approach has no common name, but it is abundantly represented in early and conservative twentieth-century compositions. In this approach tonality is a significant factor, but the concept of tonality differs from that of previous periods in that no heirarchy is recognized among the twelve tones with the single exception of the tonic. The traditional functions of the keynote are preserved, but the other eleven tones are equal, free, and independent of each other. This concept will be called *free tonality*.

There is no clear line of demarcation between free tonality and late nineteenth-century ultrachromaticism. Example 54 might be considered a borderline case. In this example all twelve notes are used, and little preference is shown for those that belong to the key, F minor. Statistically there are eighteen occurrences of the five notes out of the key and twenty-nine occurrences of the seven notes in the key. The proportions approximate those anticipated with the complete acceptance of the free tonality concept. On the other hand, a large percentage of the notes out of the key are chromatic passing tones. Only the G-flats of measures 1 and 5 and the E-naturals of measures 4 and 7 do not resolve by half step. Even these eventually arrive at their normal resolution, the G-flat with one note intervening, the E-natural with seven. The voice leading is more representative of the nineteeth century than of the twentieth century.

Ex. 54 SHOSTAKOVICH: *Symphony No. 1* (1925) p4

A more typical use of free tonality is evident in Example 55. The tonal center of F-sharp is established by the ascending fourth at the beginning and the clear cadence on that note at the end. In between, all twelve notes are used with equal freedom and independence. The conventional tendency for notes to resolve in the direction of their alteration is noticeably absent. This is to be expected, since in free tonality and the duodecuple scale there are, strictly speaking, no altered tones. In this respect the necessity of using accidentals to indicate certain pitches is misleading as they lack the conventional connotation of being raised or lowered from the basic scale. In this example the incidence of the various tones is particularly even. F-sharp and D-sharp occur most frequently—six times each, and F-natural and B-natural least—twice each. Exploiting the full duodecuple scale, Hindemith executes unusually effective approaches to the climax and the cadence.

Ex. 55 HINDEMITH: *Symphony in E-flat* (1940) p10

Melodies of this sort admittedly are more difficult to sing and remember than those in a strong conventional tonality, but once heard and learned they are equally powerful and logical. Moreover, in this style the risk of being trite and resorting to clichés is greatly reduced. This tune achieves to a high degree a sense of inevitability. Each note creates the impression of being in its proper place and indispensable, infinitely desirable characteristics in melodies of all periods and styles.

Example 56 is another illustrating the concept of free tonality. Though very different in contour from Example 55, their tonal aspects are remarkably similar with all twelve tones having equal freedom and importance in both.

Ex. 56 HINDEMITH: *Symphony in E-flat* (1940) p33

In the duodecuple scale equally tempered tuning is taken for granted, and the enharmonic spellings of notes are interchangeable. Accepted practice is to use the spelling which facilitates reading and playing, a practice Hindemith follows consistently.

Serial and nonserial atonality and free tonality are different approaches to tonal organization with the same purpose—that of exploiting the full potential of the duodecuple scale. Each in its own way occupies a significant place in contemporary music. Though there were sporadic experiments using resources beyond those of the duodecuple scale before the advent of electronic music, they exerted no real influence on the mainstreams of melodic invention. Scales with more than twelve tones to the octave and with intervals smaller than semitones are considered in Chapter 16.

Contemporary Harmonic Influence

Just as melodies of previous centuries often outlined triads and seventh chords, melodies of this century often outline contemporary harmonic structures. The influence is less obvious when the harmonies are more complex, and the trend recently has been away from melodic lines of harmonic derivation. A few melodies embodying elements of unconventional chord structures will suffice to illustrate the phenomenon.

Example 57 is one of many instances in the *Scherzo* of Bartok's *Fifth String Quartet* where the melody outlines a ninth chord.

Ex. 57 BARTOK: *String Quartet No. 5* (1934) p40

Example 58 begins with an arpeggiation of a thirteenth chord on F. In this form the harmonic influence is apparent. The thirteenth chord, however, encompasses all the notes of C major. If the notes were arranged along scale line instead of along chord line, the harmonic implication would be missing. This possibility is most apparent in thirteenth chords, but it exists in all the more complex sonorities.

Ex. 58 BRITTEN: *Peter Grimes—Interlude I* (1945) p27

Fourths, except as they resulted from inverting fifths, were dormant as harmonic ingredients from the time of organum to the present century, when the use of chords built in fourths became common practice. The fourth chord influence on the next melody, in which most of the intervals are perfect fourths, is obvious.

Ex. 59 BARTOK: *Concerto for Orchestra* (1943) p1

Example 60 has augmented and diminished as well as perfect fourths in its melodic line.

Ex. 60 BARBER: *Violin Concerto* (1941) p7

When a contemporary harmonic idiom is adopted, it is almost certain to influence the melodic writing. Such influence is both natural and desirable within limits, but interest diminishes when outlines of the prevailing sonorities are too apparent in the melodic lines. The most effective contours result when chord lines are combined with the stepwise motion of scales and nonharmonic tones.

Melodic Doubling

The doubling of melodic lines at the octave, third, and sixth is a venerable practice. To these intervals contemporary composers have added melodic doublings at other intervals and by complete chords. Doublings at conventional diatonic intervals are too common to require comment. Only doublings which color and reinforce melodic lines in less usual ways are illustrated.

The *Giuoco delle coppie* movement of Bartok's *Concerto for Orchestra* is a virtual catalog of melodic doublings. It starts, after a brief introduction on the side drum, with two bassoons playing the melody in sixths. The consistent doubling at the minor sixth, broken only once in this excerpt, produces cross (false) relations that are a characteristic feature of the passage. Examples 61–65 demonstrate that the effect of a melodic doubling is enhanced when the interval qualities deviate from those of the diatonic scale.

50

Ex. 61 BARTOK: *Concerto for Orchestra* (1943) p29

Immediately after the bassoon passage in sixths comes a section for oboes in thirds, with the minor quality predominating.

Ex. 62 BARTOK: *Concerto for Orchestra* (1943) p30

Unlike Examples 61 and 62, which are unconventional only in their emphasis on equal rather than diatonic intervals, Example 63 from the same work features doubling at a dissonant interval, the minor seventh. In any doubling at a uniform interval the two lines imply different keys.

Ex. 63 BARTOK: *Concerto for Orchestra* (1943) p30

Parallel perfect fifths, strictly forbidden by conventional rules, continue uninterrupted throughout the passage from which Example 64 is taken.

Ex. 64 BARTOK: *Concerto for Orchestra* (1943) p32

The last in this series of melodic doublings at various intervals is consecutive major seconds played by two trumpets. One not familiar with the passage might expect a dissonant effect, but the muted trumpets playing softly as they do in Example 65 produce a distinctive tone coloring which is not at all dissonant in the usual sense.

Ex. 65 BARTOK: *Concerto for Orchestra* (1943) p34

The movement from which the preceding examples were taken concludes with all five pairs of instruments playing their characteristic interval simultaneously in a D7 chord. Listening to a performance or a recording will bring these examples to life and vividly demonstrate the possibilities for contemporary melodic doubling.

Melodic doubling is not limited to single intervals. In Orff's *Catulli Carmina* the following theme is stated in parallel triads.

Ex. 66 ORFF: *Catulli Carmina* (1943) p51

A still more elaborate melodic doubling occurs in *The Rite of Spring*. The melody in octaves is paralleled by diatonic fifths and sixths above, thirds and fourths below.

Ex. 67 STRAVINSKY: *The Rite of Spring* (1913) p39

An extended melodic line in parallel ninth chords would surely be monotonous, but sonorities with ninth chord implications double melodic fragments in Example 68 with good effect. The structure of these chords is obscured by their spacing, but they can be analyzed (ignoring the pedal A's) as ninth chords with the third omitted. In each instance the three adjacent tones are the seventh, root, and ninth, and the highest tone in each hand is the fifth.

Ex. 68 DEBUSSY: *Piano Preludes, Book II No. 2—Feuilles Mortes* (1913)

Melodic doubling is a special effect used sparingly by composers to color and reinforce lines. The foregoing examples show typical applications of the device in isolated passages from larger works where it is appropriate and useful.

Suggested Assignments

1. Illustrate each distinctive twentieth-century melodic practice cited in the text with a melody copied from a contemporary composition. Other themes from the sources of the examples in the chapter may be used.
2. Write idiomatic melodies for various instruments exploiting some of the possibilities suggested in the section on nonvocal melodic lines.
3. Make a table of Messiaen's modes of limited transpositions showing each of the seven modes starting on C and on ascending semitones until the pitch content of the first transposition is repeated.
4. Analyze a passage from a Messiaen work to determine whether or not its pitches are derived from one of the modes of limited transpositions. Identify by number any modes that are detected.
5. Write melodies using scale patterns from the examples. Invent additional scales and compose melodies using them.
6. Write melodies exploiting the principles of free tonality. In these melodies pay particular attention to contour, organization, and to the element of unity which otherwise may be lacking.
7. Write melodic lines influenced by contemporary harmonic structures.
8. Listen to a recording of the second movement *(Giuoco delle coppie)* from Bartok's *Concerto for Orchestra*. Analyze the intervals between parts involved in melodic doublings by ear or from the score.
9. Devise effective doublings for original or borrowed melodies. Original melodies may be drawn from previous assignments.
10. Read "Sketch of a New Esthetic of Music" by Ferruccio Busoni in *Three Classics in the Aesthetic of Music* (Dover Publications, 1962) or in *Contemporary Composers on Contemporary Music* edited by Elliott Schwartz and Barney Childs (Holt, Rinehart and Winston, 1967).

5

Rhythm and Meter

*T*HROUGHOUT this century rhythm has been less restricted and more varied than in any prior period or style since time signatures and bar lines came into general use. These conventions of notation and the constant metric accent patterns associated with them severely inhibited rhythmic flexibility in the past. On a larger dimension the four-measure phrases which became standard were also an inhibiting factor. Though time signatures, bar lines, metric accents, and four-measure phrases are still used, their tyranny over rhythmic organization was broken early in the century by composers revolting against arbitrary restrictions and seeking means to express innovative rhythmic ideas. They devised many ways of circumventing the limitations implicit in our notational system and explored many fresh approaches to the organization of time and durations in music. Complete rhythmic freedom is now taken for granted. Cataloging all of the new devices is not feasible, but a survey of the more fruitful trends will suffice as an introduction to twentieth-century rhythm.

Nonmetric Rhythms

Traditionally, music is written in a constant meter specified by a time signature. Bar lines define metric units, and beats immediately following bar lines are accented. Music theory also establishes a heirarchy of secondary accents and unaccented beats. Generations of composers wrote music applying these principles; performers are still taught to observe them; and listeners are expected to perceive them. A wealth of music has been composed embodying these rhythmic concepts, but their limitations are obvious.

One way to circumvent such limitations is to preserve bar lines solely as a convenience of notation, disregarding in composition and performance any metric or accentual implications they formerly had. The effect is to create music without audible bar lines which is essentially nonmetric. This idea is not new. It existed in plain chant and in the vocal music of the sixteenth century. Renewed interest in sixteenth-century vocal polyphony has done much to revive it. In the absence of metric accents, notes which are approached by leap, prolonged, or embellished become functionally equivalent to the notes on metric accents, but being independent of the meter they may come any place in the measure.

The metric divisions indicated by the time signature and bar lines in Example 69 cannot be detected in performance. Ties across bar lines obliterate the metric accents and produce a subtle, free-flowing rhythm in which the phrases of seven measures and six measures sound neither irregular nor extended. The phrase divisions, which otherwise might be ambiguous, were marked by the composer as shown.

Ex. 69 HARRIS: *Symphony No. 3* (1938) p3

Example 70 illustrates the same type of rhythmic feeling, though the stresses start to coincide with the bar lines at the end. Often, as in this example, nonmetric rhythms are integrated with metrically oriented patterns. Internal repetitions create the impression of extensions, but phrase divisions are not clearly defined.

Ex. 70 SCHUMAN: *Symphony No. 3* (1941) p46

In the interpretation of nonmetric music, phrasing and articulation marks assume added importance, because the performers' instinctive responses to rhythm and those associated with metric music are not valid. Eliminating or camouflaging the effect of bar lines by ties is only one of the ways rhythmic flexibility is achieved in modern music.

Shifting Accents

Rhythmic flexibility can also be achieved by shifting accents from their normal location in the metric pattern to some other beat or fraction of a beat by means of articulation and phrasing marks that do not coincide with the metric divisions. Shifting accents can be, and frequently are, reinforced in the texture and scoring.

In the Walton example, accent marks on certain second and third beats and slurs joining pairs of quarter notes serve to shift the stresses from their normal location in the measure and to create a temporary, 2/4 meter effect.

Ex. 71 WALTON: *Symphony No. 1* (1935) p106

Accents can be displaced a fraction of a beat in conjunction with syncopated rhythms, a possibility illustrated in Example 72.

Ex. 72 STRAVINSKY: *Firebird Suite* (1910) p24

Sometimes an accent shift is associated with a rhythmic or melodic pattern that does not conform to the meter. The accents in Example 73 coincide with the repeated high points in the line but shift in relation to the beat.

Ex. 73 STRAVINSKY: *The Rite of Spring* (1913) p30

The accented beginning of the descending figure in Example 74 comes a sixteenth later in each measure.

Ex. 74 COPLAND: *Symphony No. 3* (1946) p131

Note groupings foreign to the meter are not always marked by accents. Unaccented groupings of this sort are indicated by phrasing marks or by beams joining notes within a group. Since phrasing marks also indicate bowing in string music, Schoenberg uses beams in his *String Quartet No. 4* to delineate groups of notes that extend over beats and bar lines.

Ex. 75 SCHOENBERG: *String Quartet No. 4* (1936) p59

Bowing is not a factor in the following example from a Bartok piano piece, but he beams together groups of sixteenth notes which shift position in relation to the beat. Other interpretations are possible, but the notation suggests that each group is to be played in the same way. This in effect shifts the location of any accents, real or implied, in reference to the notated beats and bar lines, which would not be perceived by listeners.

Ex. 76 BARTOK: *Mikrokosmos, No. 146—Ostinato* (1926–37)

Walton makes extensive and imaginative use of rhythmic shifts in *Belshazzar's Feast* from which Example 77 is taken. The accents do not agree with the meter or comply with any consistent pattern. On the contrary, they occur on every beat and half beat of the measure in the course of this brief excerpt.

Ex. 77 WALTON: *Belshazzar's Feast* (1931) p70

Roy Harris capitalizes on the fact that 3/2 and 6/4 measures have the same number of quarter notes but different secondary accents to write a theme with an unusual rhythm. Each measure of Example 78 fits into one pattern or the other, but mixing them adds a unique touch. The irregularly spaced accents cannot be anticipated or the location of the bar lines perceived aurally in this five-measure phrase.

Ex. 78 HARRIS: *Symphony No. 3* (1938) p56

Momentarily displaced accents producing rhythmic units of unequal duration have been illustrated in the preceding examples. When a pattern of unequal durations within a measure is used consistently, an asymmetric meter results.

Asymmetric Meters

One of the first asymmetric meters to be used was 5/4. Measures in 5/4 meter can divide either 3–2 or 2–3. Though it is not usually necessary, divisions within measures can be indicated by dotted bar lines, as Ravel does in *Daphnis and Chloe.*

Ex. 79 RAVEL: *Daphnis and Chloe, Suite No. 2* (1911) p87

Piston places the accent marks in his *Divertimento* to suggest a 2–3–2 division of the 7/8 measures.

Ex. 80 PISTON: *Divertimento* (1946) p1

The beams and slurs in the following 7/8 example imply 2–2–3 or 4–3 divisions.

Ex. 81 BARTOK: *Mikrokosmos, No. 82—Scherzo* (1926–37)

Stravinsky divides 9/8 measures asymmetrically 4–5 and then 5–4. The time signatures are shown in the example as they appear in the score.

Ex. 82 STRAVINSKY: *The Rite of Spring* (1913) p31

The measures of Example 83 contain eight eighth notes, the same number as in 4/4 meter, but the time signature explicitly groups them in an asymmetric pattern that is maintained throughout the piece.

Ex. 83 BARTOK: *Mikrokosmos, No. 153—Dance in Bulgarian Rhythm* (1926–37)

The number of eighth values in the measures of Example 84 is nine, the same as in 9/8 meter, but again Bartok specifies an asymmetric division which is constant for the entire first part of the movement from which the example is taken.

Ex. 84 BARTOK: *String Quartet No. 5* (1934) p31

In the trio of the same movement Bartok adds an eighth value to the measures for a total of ten, which he also divides asymmetrically.

Ex. 85 BARTOK: *String Quartet No. 5* (1934) p35

Many unusual time signatures are encountered in contemporary music. Several have already been illustrated. Other possibilities include the use of a small unit such as a sixteenth or a thirty-second for the beat and the use of meters which involve unusual numbers or fractions of beats. Such time signatures ordinarily have the same logical basis as conventional time signatures, and interpreting them poses no special problems. Jaques-Dalcroze conceived the idea of substituting a note symbol for the lower number in time signatures. This system is practical for any meter but is particularly advantageous when the true beat is a dotted value. Carl Orff adopted it for his *Catulli Carmina*. He writes the time signature above the staff with a line between the number and the note symbol. Hindemith uses the system intermittently in the first movement of his *Symphonia Serena*. He places the symbols on the staff like a conventional time signature, as shown.

Ex. 86 HINDEMITH: *Symphonia Serena* (1947) p4

The preceding example introduces not only a new type of time signature but also another source of rhythmic variety—changing time signatures.

Changing Time Signatures

Some of the less inspired music of the past creates the impression with its regular metric accents and evenly spaced cadences that it was written to fit into measures and phrases of standard dimensions. Not so the music of the present. Its accents are often independent of the meter, and there is no longer a viable norm for phrase lengths. Composers who elect to retain the traditional functions of time signatures and bar lines are not committed to a constant rhythmic pattern. They have the option of changing the time signature as often as necessary to reflect the metric implications of the music. Bar lines then come between beat patterns and before metric accents as in conventional music, but their placement is determined measure by measure, not in advance for an entire composition. Changing time signatures are a trademark of modern music, and virtually every score provides examples. They are an added hazard for players and conductors, but many contemporary musical ideas cannot be notated precisely within the framework of a single meter.

Frequent time signature changes may be but are not necessarily associated with complexity. Example 87 is from a simple piano piece for children.

Ex. 87 BARTOK: *For Children, Vol. 1 No. 28—Choral* (1908)

The epic *Rite of Spring* was a revolutionary work when it was written, and after more than six decades its rhythms, which involve many time changes, still sound exciting and even daring. The rhythm of Example 88 is subtle and imaginative, but not complicated.

Ex. 88 STRAVINSKY: *The Rite of Spring* (1913) p101

The *Sacrificial Dance* with which *The Rite of Spring* ends contains its most powerful and provocative rhythms. Few consecutive measures have the same time signature. The changes shown in Example 89 are representative.

Ex. 89 STRAVINSKY: *The Rite of Spring* (1913) p112

Almost any modern work will yield additional examples of variable measure lengths and metric patterns. Copland makes effective use of these devices, along with shifting accents and asymmetric meters and divisions, in *El Salón México*.

Ex. 90 COPLAND: *El Salón México* (1936) p1

New Rhythmic Concepts

The unique rhythmic concepts of Olivier Messiaen are explained in his book *The Techniques of My Musical Language*. In place of the traditional rhythmic units, beats and measures, he uses a short fractional unit such as an eighth or a sixteenth as the only constant value. Free multiplications of this fractional unit lead to a type of rhythmic organization which is essentially *ametrical*. The notation is precise but unmeasured. Bar lines do not delineate metric units but serve to mark phrase divisions and to cancel the effect of accidentals. The impression created is that of a very free rhythm, but the processes are not entirely instinctive. Some have a rational basis.

One procedure is to transform a simple rhythmic pattern by inserting a short *added value*, which can be represented by a note, a rest, or a dot. Each of these possibilities is illustrated, with the added values marked by crosses, in the following example from Messiaen's book.

Ex. 91 MESSIAEN: *Rhythms with Added Values*

Augmentation and diminution are other systematic rhythmic modifications employed extensively by Messiaen. He includes more complex multiples and fractions than the doubling and halving of the values in conventional augmentation and diminution. The following table is adapted from his book. The values on the right are the augmentations of those on the left; the values on the left are the diminutions of those on the right. The amount the durations are increased or decreased is shown beside the notation expressed as a multiple or a fraction of the original values.

Ex. 92 MESSIAEN: *Table of Augmented and Diminished Rhythms*

DIMINUTION AUGMENTATION

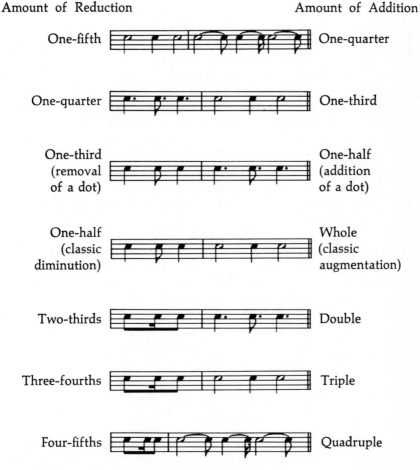

In the next example typical Messiaen rhythmic procedures are illustrated in an ametrical context. It contains added values, marked by crosses, and repetitions of a short motive augmented and diminished in turn by the addition and removal of dots.

Ex. 93 MESSIAEN: *La Nativité du Seigneur, Book IV—Dieu parmi nous* (1935)

Extract from La Nativité du Seigneur by Olivier Messiaen. Copyright by Alphonse Leduc & Cie, Paris, Owners and Publishers.

Elliot Carter is another composer with a highly individual approach to rhythm. His music is characterized by a device known as *metric modulation*. In metric modulation a proportional change of tempo is accomplished by a change from one meter to another with the two meters linked by a common value. The idea is not new, but Carter has applied it to infinitely more complex relationships than his predecessors. Those in the following passage are typical. The sixteenth-note value is constant when the time changes from 2/4 to 14/16. In the next change the beat is constant, the double-dotted-quarter note equaling the quarter note. The effect of the two changes is to reduce the tempo of the quarter-note beats from 126 to 72. After eleven measures in this tempo, the quintuplet sixteenth value becomes the sixteenth value in 10/16 meter. When the meter returns to 2/4 with the sixteenth value constant, the tempo quickens to 90 for the quarter-note beats. In Carter's equations the first note always represents the preceding tempo and the second note the following tempo. He writes a double bar line before a time signature change only when the symbol for the constant value between the two meters is different.

Ex. 94 CARTER: *Eight Etudes and a Fantasy—Fantasy* (1950)

To summarize, the expanded rhythmic resources of contemporary music include nonmetric and ametric rhythms, accents which shift in relation to the beats and bar lines, asymmetric meters, changing time signatures, added values, agumentation and diminution by unconventional ratios, and metric modulation. In addition, some twelve-tone composers have extended serial control to durations, a step in the direction of total organization. At the other end of the spectrum is aleatoric music in which durations are not specified by the composer but are determined by the performers or by chance. Electronic synthesizers and computers are capable of both ultimate precision and random selection in rhythmic matters, but the notation (if any) is usually no more than a graphic, second-by-second schedule of sound events. These newest styles are considered further under their respective headings.

Practical young composers, unless working with electronic media, are well advised to use rhythmic devices which will intrigue but not discourage the players who are available to perform their music. Excessively difficult rhythms are an insurmountable barrier to group performance by any but the most expert and experienced players. Besides, some of the most effective rhythms are those which make only minor but striking departures from convention.

Suggested Assignments

1. Locate and copy examples illustrating the categories of contemporary rhythm discussed in this chapter. Analyze the phrase structures of the longer examples.
2. Write a paper describing and categorizing the rhythmic procedures in a contemporary work you have played or sung. Illustrate your comments with appropriate examples.
3. Write a melody with nonmetric rhythm similar in style to Examples 69 and 70.
4. Write an exercise in which accents shift in relation to the bar lines and/or beats.
5. Write an exercise in an asymmetric meter.
6. Write an exercise in which time changes are exploited as a characteristic feature.
7. Write an exercise featuring added values in an ametrical context.
8. Compose a piece for a percussion instrument or ensemble in which frequent tempo changes are accomplished by means of metric modulation.
9. Compose a short piece exploring a variety of contemporary rhythmic devices.
10. For additional reading on rhythm see Paul Creston's book *Principles of Rhythm* (Franco Colombo, 1964).

6

Chord Structure

CHORD structure is the vertical arrangement of notes sounding simultaneously. Harmonic sounds rarely occur in isolation, but a thorough understanding of chord structure is necessary before considering the more complicated problem of harmonic progression. Knowledge of conventional chord structures, including all of the triads and seventh chords with their inversions and alterations, is presumed. This chapter is concerned with the more complex sonorities required to express most contemporary musical ideas. This need, and not the search for novelty which is sometimes suspected, has caused the tremendous expansion in the harmonic vocabulary of our time.

When first hearing music in advanced twentieth-century harmonic idioms, one sometimes gets the impression that modern composers have severed all ties with tradition and the traditional music which makes up the bulk of concert programs, broadcasts, and recordings. This break is more apparent than real. The development of harmonic resources has followed a consistent course of exploiting higher and higher elements of the overtone series. In this respect contemporary composers are merely continuing a process that started with organum and magadizing and led successively to triads and chords of the seventh, ninth, eleventh, thirteenth, and beyond. The enrichment of harmonic resources through the successive inclusion of higher members of the overtone series is shown in the following example.

Though more complex chords were used sporadically before the turn of the century, the most active chord fully accepted was the dominant seventh, which is produced by the first seven tones of the overtone series. Within two decades sonorities comprising the most remote relationships were an integral part of every composer's harmonic language. The speed with which new sounds were introduced obscured the fact that they were the inevitable result of the evolutionary process. It is worth noting that even relatively simple dissonant chords such as the dominant minor ninth involve tonal relationships which do not exist within the first sixteen overtones.

Ex. 95 OVERTONE SERIES

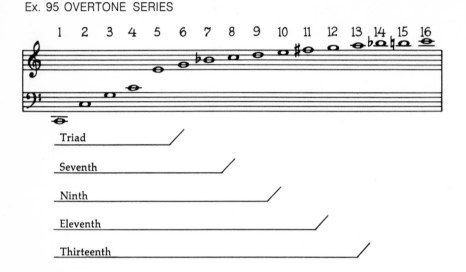

The pitches of some overtones, seven and eleven among them, are only approximated in equally tempered tuning, but because of its practical advantages equal temperament has been adopted universally, at least as far as keyboard instruments and notation are concerned. One advantage of equal temperament is that it permits the use of enharmonic spellings to facilitate reading and as used in this chapter, to simplify anaylsis.

In the following examples representative chord structures selected from twentieth-century works are given, usually in brief context. When required to make the underlying chord structure more apparent, the components are arranged in root position with close spacing and enharmonic spellings. Corresponding numbers identify the chords under consideration and their simplified versions shown in whole notes. This type of analyisis and description is used in the absence of any convenient, standard terminology for modern chord formations.

Superimposed Thirds

Contemporary chords built in thirds are most closely related to conventional harmonies since they continue the process by which triads and seventh chords are constructed, superimposition of thirds. The study of conventional harmony usually encompasses all diatonic triad and seventh chord structures in major and minor keys though some of them, such as minor and augmented triads with major sevenths, are rare in traditional music. Chromatic alteration was used prior to the present century to make various chord structures available on each degree of the scale but not to create new harmonic formations.

Chromatic alteration of the notes in conventional seventh chords can produce new structures like that of the first chord in Example 96. Observe how effectively this chord progresses to the dominant seventh.[1] The B-flat in the last chord of the example appears in the score as a B-flat and also enharmonically as an A-sharp. Either way it is an unconventional spelling of a familiar sound.

Ex. 96 BARTOK: *Piano Concerto No. 3* (1945) p10

There are several other possibilities for seventh chord structures which do not occur diatonically. One favored by Gershwin consists of a diminished triad with a major seventh. Unfortunately, examples from Gershwin cannot be given because of copyright restrictions.

The addition of a third above the seventh produces a ninth chord. This structure was first used on the fifth degree of the scale, that is, as a dominant ninth. It soon became common on other scale degrees. Diatonically, the ninth of the dominant is major in major keys and minor in minor keys. Both forms figured prominently in early twentieth-century music, especially in the music of impressionist composers. Example 97 shows the dominant major ninth structure in its most usual arrangement, with the root in the bass and the ninth in the soprano.

---

1. Dominant seventh in this sense denotes a chord structure of a major triad and a minor seventh, not dominant function in a key.

Ex. 97 DEBUSSY: *Pelleas and Melisande* (1902) p7

Other inversions and positions of ninth chords, such as those shown in Example 98, are not uncommon. Each chord contains a ninth, but probably only the one in the first and third measures would be perceived as a ninth chord. The one in the second measure is more apt to be heard as a whole-tone dominant seventh on A.

Ex. 98 DEBUSSY: *Pelleas and Melisande* (1902) p78

The next example, from a nonimpressionist choral work, shows a major seventh chord progressing to a major ninth chord.

Ex. 99 KODALY: *Te Deum* (1936) p8

The dominant minor ninth is illustrated in Example 100. The last chord has the third spelled enharmonically as G-flat. The fifths of ninth chords are frequently omitted, as they are here.

Ex. 100 BLOCH: *Violin Sonata No. 1* (1920) p60

Ninths are added to chord structures other than the dominant seventh. Example 101 has two ninth chords, the first with a minor third.

Ex. 101 TCHEREPNIN: *Bagatelles, Op. 5 No. 1* (1918)

The harmonic implication of the first measure in Example 102 seems to be a ninth chord on F-sharp. Though the notes do not occur simultaneously, all appear and only the D-sharp is foreign to this chord. A dominant ninth on E and its resolution occupy the second measure, with the C-sharp sounding like a free anticipation or a thirteenth.

Ex. 102 RAVEL: *Piano Sonatine* (1905) p3

Ninth chords frequently appear in passages where tonality is vague. In such passages they gain in interest and in freedom of progression. Ninth chords contribute to the dissipation of tonality when they do not resolve in a conventional manner. This is especially true when they progress by parallel motion to another ninth chord. Example 103 illustrates this usage.

Ex. 103 DEBUSSY: *Piano Preludes, Book II No. 2—Feuilles Mortes* (1913)

The ninth chord on C-sharp in Example 104 has the structure but not the function of a dominant. The G-sharp minor chord following it has a ninth, A-sharp, but technically is not a ninth chord, because it lacks a seventh.

Ex. 104 HANSON: *Lament for Beowulf* (1925) p36

When the fifth of a major ninth chord is lowered a semitone, a whole-tone ninth chord like the one in Example 105 results. The lowered fifth, D-flat, is also written enharmonically as C-sharp.

Ex. 105 DEBUSSY: *Piano Preludes, Book II No. 10—Canope* (1913)

Ninth chords, especially nondominant ninths, can be spaced in ways that obscure their underlying structure, as in Example 106. The ear can scarcely detect the tertial derivation of these sonorities. The perception of chord 2 as a ninth chord is complicated by the major seventh and the omission of the third.

Ex. 106 RAVEL: *Piano Concerto in G* (1931) p95

The examples show only a few of the many possible ninth chords. Major and minor ninths can be added to all of the seventh chord structures, both diatonic and altered. The dominant ninth was the first to be incorporated into the harmonic vocabulary, but its value to serious composers is impaired by popular connotations and triteness. The pungent sounds of other less hackneyed ninth chord forms are still capable of expressiveness, even to jaded twentieth-century ears, when used with imagination.

The addition of another third above a ninth produces an eleventh chord. Like ninth chords, eleventh chords first appeared on the fifth degree of the scale as dominants, but subsequently were employed on other scale degrees and in other forms. Example 107 is a strong, tonal cadence in C-major with a supertonic eleventh and a dominant eleventh progressing to a tonic with an added sixth. The spacing of the score is preserved in the reduction.

Ex. 107 STRAVINSKY: *Petrouchka* (1911) p56

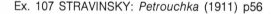

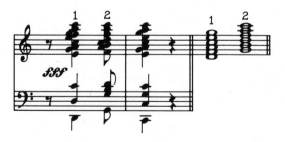

The elevenths in the preceding example are diatonic, but the sharp or augmented eleventh is more resonant. Actually, the pitch of the eleventh tone of the overtone series is between that of the diatonic and augmented eleventh in equal temperament. Example 108 has the augmented eleventh with a minor ninth, written enharmonically as C-sharp in the violin part for easier reading. The omission of the chord fifth in this example and in similar structures does not alter the sound appreciably.

Ex. 108 BLOCH: *Violin Sonata No. 1* (1920) p23

The examples illustrate typical eleventh chords, but elevenths can be added to all of the ninth chord structures. Experimentation will reveal which alterations, spacing, and inversions are most effective.

Continuing the process of chord building in thirds leads ultimately to thirteenth chords, which have one more third than eleventh chords. A diatonic thirteenth chord contains every note of the scale, but more often than not there is some chromatic alteration. A thirteenth chord with an augmented eleventh, illustrated in Example 109, is a common form.

Ex. 109 RAVEL: *Piano Concerto in G* (1931) p73

Bloch utilizes an identical structure in his *Violin Sonata*. Three versions of the same basic chord are illustrated in Example 110. The first and second are from adjoining passages; the third from the following movement.

Ex. 110 BLOCH: *Violin Sonata No. 1* (1920)

a. p42

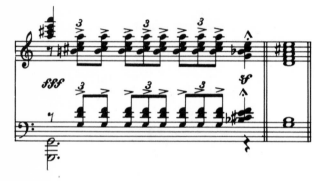

b. p43

c. p49

As with the other tertial sonorities, thirteenths can be added to all of the chord structures previously considered. Inclusion of seven tones in a single chord allows almost infinite variation in spacing, inversion, and alteration producing many degrees of resonance and dissonance. Since a thirteenth chord consists of a complete circle of thirds, any tonal member may be considered the root from a standpoint of abstract structure. For this reason the true root can be determined only on the basis of the sound. Consequently the bass most often is perceived as the root when thirds predominate in the spacing. When the chord members are arranged to emphasize seconds and fourths, which is equally possible, the same notes may be quite lacking in tertial implication.

The tone a third above the thirteenth is a duplication of the root two octaves higher. To construct chords in thirds beyond the thirteenth, one must resort to double inflections. That is, a natural note and the same note with a flat or sharp must be used. Double inflections are not uncommon, but tertial sonorities with all seven tones plus double inflections are extremely rare and of limited usefulness. They are found in isolated passages of a few works such as Gershwin's *Porgy and Bess*.

Students accustomed to writing within the bounds of academic harmony discover a new and exciting realm in ninth, eleventh, and thirteenth chords. This threshold is not crossed without forfeiting some advantages of simple chord structures. The essential characteristics of conventional chords remain intact through a wide range of inversions, spacings, and doublings. This is less true of even slightly more dissonant harmonies. Formulation of precise rules applicable to all complex sonorities is not possible, but the overtone series provides a convenient and generally valid guide. Complicated chords are most resonant in root position with wider intervals below and narrower intervals above, as they occur in the overtone series. Within this spacing greater resonance results when the lower partials of the chord root are toward the bass and the higher partials are toward the soprano, approximating their location in the series. Other arrangements tend to inhibit the resonance and sharpen the dissonance of any tonal combination. Distributing chord members according to the overtone series is merely a rule of thumb, not an inviolable principle. Unusual inversions and spacings are required on occasion to produce a desired effect. In the final analysis composers rely on their ears, imagination, and taste in these matters as in all compositional decisions.

Chords of more than four tones, not counting octave doublings, are inclined to be thick and cumbersome, and nothing palls faster than a composition overladen with ninth, eleventh, and thirteenth chords. A more serious problem is that such chords virtually eliminate the possibility of vigorous counterpoint. Every note of a seven-tone scale is contained in a thirteenth chord, so melodic lines within the key can only go from one chord tone to another. Notes outside the key, being no more than a semitone from one of the chord tones, merely sound like neighboring tones. Because of these limitations, such lush sounds have long been out of vogue. Related sonorities which preserve their advantages and avoid their shortcomings are better suited to modern requirements.

Chords of Addition and Omission

These apparently contradictory terms are applied to a group of closely related sonorities. Many of the chords falling in these classifications may be analyzed in either way, depending upon the point of view, as will be shown in the analysis. A simple chord to which is added one or more notes normally foreign but used as an integral part of the sonority is designated a *chord of addition*. A more complex chord from which one or more normally essential elements is omitted is designated a *chord of omission*. Added and omitted notes are identified by the interval above the root of the basic chord.

The most obvious example of a chord of addition is the *tonic added sixth*, the chord on which *The Song of the Earth* ends.

Ex. 111 MAHLER: *The Song of the Earth* (1908) p159

A supertonic seventh chord in the first inversion has the same structure as a tonic added sixth, but when the function is clearly tonic as in the preceding example, the only plausible analysis is as a chord of addition. The tonic added sixth has been appropriated by composers and arrangers of popular music, but it is still a valid manifestation of a process by which many other sonorities are constructed.

Triads with added seconds are also found in popular music, but their popular connotations are less disqualifying. The half-note chord in the following example could be analyzed as a ninth chord with the seventh omitted, but analyzing it as a major triad with an added second (ninth) seems preferable. The omission of the seventh significantly alters the effect of a ninth. If, on the other hand, the fifth were omitted instead of the seventh, the effect would be very close to that of a complete ninth chord.

Ex. 112 KODALY: *Te Deum* (1936) p15

In Example 113 a sixth and a second are added to a major triad.

Ex. 113 HARRIS: *American Ballads, No. 1* (1947)

A minor triad with an added second is equally effective.

Ex. 114 DEBUSSY: *Pelleas and Melisande* (1902) p6

Example 115 shows a major triad with an added second progressing to a
dominant thirteenth with the eleventh omitted, which can also be analyzed as a dominant ninth with an added sixth.

Ex. 115 DEBUSSY: *Piano Preludes, Book II No. 10—Canopes* (1913)

In tertial harmonies the omission of the third evokes the greatest
change. If the bass notes are analyzed as the roots, the chords in Example
116 are ninth chords with the thirds omitted. The chords can also be
analyzed as major triads with added perfect fourths. The added notes
in this case are below the triads, unlike those in any of the previous examples. Since notes are most often added above the basic chord and the
octave doubling suggests root function for the bass notes, the analysis as
chords of omission is more convincing.

Ex. 116 COPLAND: *Violin Sonata* (1943) p13

Added notes are not necessarily in a diatonic relationship to the underlying chord. Any note can be added. A major triad with an added augmented fourth, both spelled enharmonically in the analysis for greater clarity, is shown in Example 117.

Ex. 117 KODALY: *Te Deum* (1936) p13

The first chord in Orff's *Catulli Carmina* is a minor triad with an added augmented fourth.

Ex. 118 ORFF: *Catulli Carmina* (1943) p1

A more sophisticated added-note chord is used by Bloch to close the second movement of his *Violin Sonata*. After firmly establishing the key of B-flat minor, he uses a tonic added sixth for the cadence chord, subsequently adding a major seventh and an augmented fourth.

Ex. 119 BLOCH: *Violin Sonata No. 1* (1920) p47

Sometimes an added note is another inflection of a basic chord member as in Example 120. The chords have both major and minor thirds with the minor thirds above the major thirds, which is usual.

Ex. 120 BRITTEN: *Peter Grimes—Prologue* (1945) p2

Three chords of addition or omission over the same root are used in Example 121: a minor triad with an added second, a dominant seventh structure with an added minor third, and a thirteenth chord with the third and eleventh omitted.

Ex. 121 HARRIS: *American Ballads, No. 4* (1947)

These examples show some typical chords of addition and omission. Many more are possible, and this process places at the disposal of the composer an infinite variety of sonorities with an unusually wide range of consonance and dissonance. Sonorities of this type have the added advantage of a close link with tradition in their underlying basic chord. Sounds with a perceptible relation to conventional chords have more appeal for typical listeners than obtuse tonal combinations, an advantage not to be overlooked by composers still seeking recognition and without assured performances.

When three notes or more are added to a chord, they more often than not assume the form of another chord. This leads to the next classification of harmonic sounds, those that result from combining simple chords.

Polychords

Sonorities which can best be understood as combinations of conventional chords are designated *polychords*. Only triads and seventh chords are united in polychordal formations. Less familiar structures lose their identity in complex associations. The elements of individual chords within a polychord are united with each other and isolated from those of other chords by spacing, register, and/or color to emphasize the distinctive polychordal quality.

Every seventh chord is in a sense a combination of two triads. For example, the dominant seventh chord on G can be analyzed as a G major triad combined with a B diminished triad. All seventh chords can be regarded as combinations of various types of triads with roots a third apart. According to this method of analysis each ninth chord encompasses three triads and two seventh chords. Eleventh chords encompass four triads, three seventh chords, and two ninth chords, and thirteenth chords encompass five triads, four seventh chords, three ninth chords, and two eleventh chords. As long as there are common tones and a close relationship between the triads, they are perceived as components of a single chord unless widely separated in register or scored in contrasting colors. The polychordal implications of such chords can be stressed deliberately by spacing and scoring.

Though interesting polychordal effects are possible with the components of ninth, eleventh, and thirteenth chords, most polychords combine elements of two keys or modes. One such polychord, consisting of two major triads in the tritone relationship, permeates Stravinsky's *Petrouchka* and provides a strong unifying element in the complete work. While trumpets and cornets play the C major figure in Example 122, horns sustain the F-sharp major triad, and strings, woodwinds, and piano play the two triads in rapid alternation. Significantly, all of the pitches in this passage are from the octatonic scale (see p. 42) on C, which has the same pitch content as the octatonic scale on F-sharp.

Ex. 122 STRAVINSKY: *Petrouchka* (1911) p60

The sonority resulting from two major triads at the distance of a tritone
is not so remote from those considered previously as might be expected.
The sounds of Example 122 can be rearranged and spelled enharmonically
as a dominant minor ninth with an augmented eleventh.

Ex. 123

The visual impression of complex chords can be changed by enharmonic spellings. The spelling of a particular chord is influenced by the
way it is used, and the analysis is influenced in turn by the spelling. Such
distinctions are of no great importance when dealing with isolated harmonic structures, but the spelling used by the composer is taken into account in the following analyses. The reductions are designed to reveal the
underlying structure. Other interpretations are possible in some cases.

Hanson uses the augmented fourth relationship between two dominant
seventh type chords in his *Romantic Symphony*. The chord is scored for
full orchestra with the spacing shown first.

Ex. 124 HANSON: *Symphony No. 2 "Romantic"* (1930) p39

The tritone is only one of the possible polychord relationships. Harris makes an effective final cadence with major triads on roots a major third apart.

Ex. 125 HARRIS: *American Ballads, No. 4* (1947)

Ravel uses a G major triad and a D-sharp minor seventh chord together in a piano figuration.

Ex. 126 RAVEL: *Piano Concerto in G* (1931) p1

Later in the same work a minor triad and a major triad with roots a major seventh apart are combined in a polychord. Spelling the third of the lower triad as B-flat and the third of the upper triad as A-sharp, as Ravel does, confirms the polychord analysis even though all six notes can be arranged in ascending thirds.

Ex. 127 RAVEL: *Piano Concerto in G* (1931) p91

In Example 128 contrary motion between major triads produces poly-chords with varied root relationships—major seventh, perfect fifth, major third, and major second. Triads with roots a fifth and a seventh apart produce chords which can be analyzed as ninth and eleventh chords respectively, but in this instance the polychord analysis is supported by the harmonic streams.

Ex. 128 SCHUMAN: *Three-Score Set, No. 2* (1943)

One of the most complex polychords occurs in *The Rite of Spring* where a major triad and a dominant seventh structure with roots a major seventh apart are combined. The scoring is homogeneous. The complete polychord in the spacing shown is played by divisi strings reinforced on the accents by eight horns. After eight measures of the block chord,

broken forms of these same two chords (F-flat major now spelled enharmonically as E major) are combined with a third chord—a C major triad.

Ex. 129 STRAVINSKY: *The Rite of Spring* (1913) p11

The process of combining triads and seventh chords in polychords adds
a new dimension to the harmonic pallette. This means of constructing
sonorities has the potential for an unlimited range of dissonance and
resonance. As with most complex chord structures the effect depends as
much upon position, spacing, register, and scoring as upon pitch content.
In these matters the overtone series is a less efficient guide for polychords,
since they draw material from two sources, than for tertial chord structures. Testing various polychord combinations at the piano provides experience in selecting effective relationships, spacings, and registers.
Studying scores and listening to recordings of works containing polychords serve to illustrate the effects of orchestral coloring in the absence of
opportunities to experiment with an instrumental ensemble.

Nontertial Sonorities

Chords built in superimposed thirds have been studied along with
various additions to and combinations of such chords. Another fertile
source of twentieth-century harmonic material is chord construction by
intervals other than thirds. Chords constructed of other intervals are considered collectively as *nontertial sonorities.*

Nontertial sonorities are not without ancestors in more conventional
chords. The second inversion of a triad with a seven-six suspension in
the soprano gives a chord in fourths. When the seventh, root, and ninth
of a ninth chord appear in close position in that order, a segment of a
chord in seconds results. The thirteenth chord, since it contains all of
the tones of a seven-tone scale, can be arranged in seconds, fourths, and
fifths as well as in thirds. Regarded in this way nontertial sonorities rep-

resent a logical manner of extending harmonic resources along lines suggested in more conventional harmonies and sometimes existing in
embryonic form in traditional practices.

Some of the earliest nontertial sonorities resulted when four-note
chords were derived from a whole-tone scale, since only augmented triads
can be produced by alternate scale tones. The nontertial structure of
chord 1 in Example 130 is apparent. Chord 2 appears to be tertial, but one
of the thirds is diminished and sounds like a major second. Actually, the
two chords have the same underlying structure, a fact which becomes
apparent if the pitches of the first chord are rearranged and spelled enharmonically—F, A, C-sharp, E-flat. This spacing and spelling reveals a
structure like a dominant seventh chord with a raised fifth, the so-called
whole-tone dominant.

Ex. 130 DEBUSSY: *Pelleas and Melisande* (1902) p3

After one conventional dominant seventh chord, Example 131 consists
of a series of whole-tone dominants. While the last one is sustained, an
F-sharp is added in the bass and a D appears in the repeated note figure,
so all six notes of the whole-tone scale are sounding simultaneously.

Ex. 131 DEBUSSY: *Piano Preludes, Book I No. 6—Des Pas sur la Neige* (1910)

Chords in seconds are not used only by impressionist composers or derived exclusively from whole-tone scales. Seconds are prominent in the harmonies of Example 132 though the sustained notes in the violin part perhaps should be regarded as pedal tones rather than chord tones.

Ex. 132 COPLAND: *Violin Sonata* (1943) p13

Seconds are used in a different fashion in Example 133.

Ex. 133 BARTOK: *Mikrokosmos, No. 107—Melody in the Mist* (1926–37)

Chords of three or more consecutive seconds are known as *clusters*. The first clusters were conceived in terms of the piano, for which they are idiomatic, but soon they were being used in music for other mediums (see p 232). Example 134 shows seven-note clusters on the white keys alternating rapidly with the five black-key notes, together comprising all twelve tones of a chromatic octave.

Ex. 134 BARTOK: *Piano Concerto No. 2* (1931) p57

Clusters with more notes and a wider compass are illustrated in the excerpt from the accompaniment of a Charles Ives song.

Ex. 135 IVES: *114 Songs—Majority* (1922)

Composer's Edition[2]

Henry Cowell's piano compositions which he performed in public for the first time in 1912 included clusters, for which he devised a special system of notation. The symbols shown in Example 136 indicate that all of the keys, black and white, between the upper and lower notes are to be played simultaneously using both forearms.

Ex. 136 COWELL: *Piano Music, No. 8—Tiger* (1928)

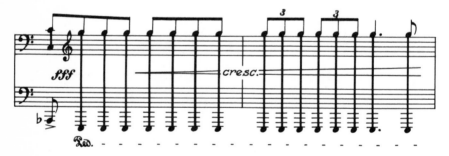

Associated Music Publishers, Inc., New York.

Strangely enough, such tonal conglomerates as these are not perceived as dissonant in the usual sense. They neither sound active nor demand resolution, but integrated with other types of chords they add a provocative contemporary ingredient. In some more recent works the basic texture is essentially a massive cluster. This is true of Xenakis's *Metastasis*

---

2. A fascimile of the original edition was produced in 1970 by University Microfilms, Ann Arbor, Michigan. "Majority" is also included in *Nineteen Songs* by Charles Ives published by Merion Music, Inc., Theodore Presser Company, Sole Representative.

(1955) in which a continuously evolving sound mass is produced by 61 instrumentalists playing 61 totally independent parts.

Contemporary composers also make use of sonorities in which fourths are the primary interval. Fourth chords generally lack the resonance of tertial sonorities, because their components are not as closely related to the overtones of the root and consequently are reinforced less by them. This is particularly true when all of the fourths are perfect and when fourths are the only intervals in the structure. Fourth chords are not ordinarily used throughout a composition or even for extended passages, but they are a prize harmonic resource for intermittent use and brief passages.

La Cathédrale Engloutie is a familiar work in which fourth chords are used extensively. Fourths predominate in all of the chords of Example 137 except the third of the quarter-note chords. Observe that seconds result from octave doublings in fourth chords.

Ex. 137 DEBUSSY: *Piano Preludes, Book I No. 10—La Cathédrale Engloutie* (1910)

When one of the fourths in a fourth chord is inverted and becomes a fifth, as in the whole-note chord of the preceding example, the lower member asserts itself as the root and tends to create the impression of a tertial sonority with the third omitted. For this reason the fifth directly above the bass is avoided when the distinctive fourth-chord quality is desired.

Berg runs the gamut of chords in perfect fourths, from two notes to seven, in *Wozzeck*. Since all of the motion in Example 138 is parallel, perhaps it should be considered merely melodic doubling. It cannot be regarded as a typical example of chord progression, but it illustrates with unusual clarity extended structures in perfect fourths, though some are notated as augmented thirds.

Ex. 138 BERG: *Wozzeck—Act I Scene 4* (1914–21) p70

A more varied use of fourth chords is shown in Example 139. The basic chords are built in perfect fourths, with contrary motion and moving parts adding interest.

Ex. 139 IVES: *114 Songs—Majority* (1922)

Composer's Edition[3]

---

3. See fn. p. 96.

Though it hardly would be suspected from the sound, the final chord in the Schoenberg piano piece is written in fourths, one of them perfect and the other two augmented. Chords containing augmented or diminished fourths bear little resemblance in sound to those constructed in perfect fourths.

Ex. 140 SCHOENBERG: *Three Piano Pieces, Op. 11 No. 1* (1910)

Scriabin's celebrated "mystic" chord has an unusually interesting structure consisting of perfect, augmented, and diminished fourths as shown at the end of Example 141. Most of the notes in this excerpt, and indeed in the entire piece, are derived from the generating "mystic" chord in various transpositions.

Ex. 141 SCRIABIN: *Poème, Op. 69 No. 1* (1913)

P. Jurgenson, Moscow[4]

Chords built entirely in fifths are rare, but they do occur. One such instance is in *The Rite of Spring* where the following six-note chord in perfect fifths is used.

---

4. Also available in a Peters edition.

Ex. 142 STRAVINSKY: *The Rite of Spring* (1913) p13

The first chord of Example 143 has the same structure as the preceding example, after which the harmony breaks into two streams of three-note chords in fifths in contrary motion.

Ex. 143 BARTOK: *Piano Concerto No. 2* (1931) p44

The final chord of Example 144 is another six-note chord in fifths, one of them diminished. The notes of the left hand must be placed above those of the right hand to realize the fifth spacing throughout.

Ex. 144 SCHOENBERG: *Three Piano Pieces, Op. 11 No. 2* (1910)

Chord structures featuring perfect fourths and fifths are used in the *Lament for Beowulf* to evoke the archaic atmosphere of the text. Only an outline of the harmony is given. In the original these chords are repeated in a rhythmic pattern as a background to the vocal lines.

Ex. 145 HANSON: *Lament for Beowulf* (1925) p6

A chord in fourths progresses to a chord in fifths in Example 146. Only melody notes sounding at the time the chord is struck are included in the analysis.

Ex. 146 SCHOENBERG: *Three Piano Pieces, Op. 11 No. 2* (1910)

Example 147 which shows the harmonic outline of a section of a Bartok quartet, employs some conventional structures and some discussed in this chapter between a chord in fifths and a chord in fourths. Directly below the original doubling and spacing of the chords, their components are arranged to reveal the underlying structures.

Ex. 147 BARTOK: *String Quartet No. 5* (1934) p50

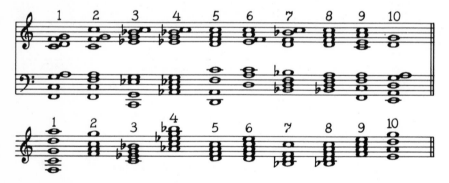

It is when diverse harmonic structures are exploited in succession, as they are in Example 147, rather than when types are isolated that maximum effectiveness is achieved. Though this fact cannot be adequately illustrated in brief examples, it would be obvious if the complete works were examined.

Suggested Assignments

1. Reduce the harmonic structures in Debussy's *La Cathédrale Engloutie (Piano Preludes, Book I no. 10)* to their simplest form and classify them according to the categories used in this chapter.
2. Analyze selected excerpts from Stravinsky's *Petrouchka* in the manner of Assignment 1. Examples 107 and 122 can serve as points of departure.
3. Locate distinctive chords in contemporary compositions and arrange their components to reveal the underlying structures.
4. Write chords illustrating each category discussed in this chapter. For each basic structure devise several effective arrangements with varied spacing and doubling and in different registers and inversions.
5. For additional reading on chord structure see Howard Hanson's *Harmonic Materials of Modern Music* (Appleton-Century-Crofts, 1960).

7

Harmonic Progression

T HE chord structures explored in Chapter 6 are like individual words. As the full significance of words is realized when they are joined with other words in sentences, the full significance of chords is realized when they are joined with other chords in progressions.

Harmonic progression, like harmonic structure, is characterized by unlimited freedom in twentieth-century music. The prohibitions of traditional harmony texts and the principles scrupulously observed by composers of the common practice period are not valid for contemporary styles. Early in the century music reached a point where every harmonic relationship as well as every chord structure was allowed and accepted. This chapter is concerned with harmonic progressions that depart from tradition in logical ways which yield to analysis.

To understand and appreciate the change of attitude regarding harmonic relationships, the old and the new must be compared. During the period when much of the familiar music literature was composed, major-minor tonality and the concepts of chord inversion and fundamental bass (codified by Jean-Philippe Rameau in 1722) dominated musical thinking. Major-minor tonality implies rather strict adherence to two seven-tone scale patterns with certain triad and seventh-chord structures associated with each scale degree. The variety inherent in the three forms of minor was reduced by the preference for the harmonic form which borrowed the critical leading tone feature from major. These scales and the principles associated with them determined the basic chord structures and functional relationships. Any others occurred incidentally and in supporting roles.

A strong sense of tonality was fostered during the tonal period by emphasis upon chord root movements in fourths and fifths, the relationships most conducive to tonality. Limitations are never apparent in a masterpiece. One is not conscious of the fact that Mozart was working within what would now be regarded as the confines of the major-minor system. It is a tribute to his genius that he created such monumental works with so few resources and perhaps a recognition of our own limitations that motivates our perpetual quest for new ones.

Even during the relatively stable tonal period, harmonic concepts were evolving continually, if slowly. The process accelerated during the romantic era, and just before the turn of the century the revolution began.

To facilitate comprehension of contemporary harmonic progressions, they are considered here in various categories and in connection with the simpler chord structures. In actual usage no such isolation exists, and all of the progressions and relationships are possible with sophisticated as well as with simple structures.

Modal Quality

In matters of harmony, as of melody, modern composers have not overlooked the modes in their search for fresh resources. Since the earlier uses of modal materials were largely melodic and contrapuntal, their harmonic possibilities were not exhausted, and at the beginning of the century the modes provided a ready means for extending the horizons of tonal organization. Some passages are purely modal, while others merely display evidence of modal influence.

The modes do not make available any chord structure not found in major and minor. The differences are in the relationships between chords and in their functions. In the major-minor system chromatic notes and altered chords traditionally resolve in prescribed ways. The result is that voice leading and harmonic progressions become stereotyped. These traditions no doubt stem from conditioning more than from any inherent inclination, but they constitute a force that must be reckoned with in writing for audiences indoctrinated with tonal practices. By making the same sounds available with diatonic notes, the modes provide an effective antidote for tonal conventions and release harmonic progressions from onerous encumbrances.

Each mode offers a different set of diatonic harmonic values, thereby multiplying the number of subtle harmonic relationships possible without resorting to chromatic alteration and submitting to its attendant restrictions. Use of the modes additionally tends to negate the tyrannical dominant-tonic relationship of tonal music, especially in modes having a minor dominant. In each mode there are three major triads, three minor triads, and one diminished triad, but the order is different. The following table gives the disposition of the various triad qualities in the seven diatonic modes.

TRIAD QUALITY IN THE MODES

Mode	Tonic	Supertonic	Mediant	Subdominant	Dominant	Submediant	Subtonic
Ionian	major	minor	minor	major	major	minor	diminished
Dorian	minor	minor	major	major	minor	diminished	major
Phrygian	minor	major	major	minor	diminished	major	minor
Lydian	major	major	minor	diminished	major	minor	minor
Mixolydian	major	minor	diminished	major	minor	minor	major
Aeolian	minor	diminished	major	minor	minor	major	major
Locrian	diminished	major	minor	minor	major	major	minor

Just as each mode has a distinctive pattern of triad relationships, each has a unique arrangement of seventh chord qualities and all other harmonic structures. The following examples illustrate some of the ways modal resources have been tapped by contemporary composers. The primary concern at this point is to show a variety of relationships in chord quality through the use of the modes, but observe that freedom also extends to the root relationships.

In Example 148 the violin melody, which is a fugue subject, is pure Dorian on C-sharp. The A's in the piano part are natural rather than sharp, making its mode Aeolian. The octave B-sharps which occur in the sequential third measure are foreign to the mode but normal leading tones in harmonic minor.

Ex. 148 BARTOK: *Piano Concerto No. 3* (1943) p55

The Phrygian mode on G is illustrated in Example 149. The mode is pure except for the F-sharp in the penultimate chord, and even there the characteristic minor second degree of the scale, A-flat, is retained.

Ex. 149 DEBUSSY: *String Quartet* (1893) p1

Because the Lydian mode is similiar in effect to major, it is difficult to isolate. The characteristic augmented fourth degree of the Lydian scale occurs so frequently as a chromatic note in major that differentiation between them is problematical. Example 150 is typical. The tonal center is A, and both D-sharp and D-natural are used. Ignoring the key signature, either could be regarded as the diatonic scale tone. The repeated D-sharps in measure 9 and in the descending figure in measures 12–14 impart a Lydian flavor to the passage, and the D-naturals can be explained in each case as chromatic nonchord tones.

Ex. 150 SIBELIUS: *Symphony No. 4 in Am* (1911) p38

Unlike Lydian, the Mixolydian mode with its characteristic minor seventh degree and minor dominant is readily distinguished from major, as it is in Example 151. Adler's *Capriccio* for piano has no key signature, but the B-flats and E-flats required for Mixolydian on F are added consistently. The 6/8 and 7/8 measures are modulatory. The restatement of the first phrase a third higher with its mirror is again pure Mixolydian.

Ex. 151 ADLER: *Capriccio* (1954)

The Aeolian mode exists in conventional music theory as natural minor, but it is rarely used in the music of the common practice period. Whether the mode of Example 152 is identified as Aeolian or natural minor is of no consequence. The E-naturals in measures 8 and 9 are used in a way that suggests borrowing from Dorian rather than melodic minor.

Ex. 152 MENOTTI: *The Medium* (1946) p48

Melodies in the Locrian mode are rare, and because of the diminished quality of its tonic triad, harmonies in this mode are even rarer. Example 153 is an instance of Locrian if D is accepted as the tonal center. The problem of the diminished tonic triad is solved by dropping the upper voices and cadencing on D alone. G may be heard as the tonal center, in which case the mode is Phrygian.

Ex. 153 BRITTEN: *A Ceremony of Carols, No. 8* (1942)

The quality relationships available within the individual modes are only the beginning. When the chord qualities of major, minor and all of the modes are used interchangeably, the potential for variety becomes almost infinite.

Change of Mode/Free Quality and Root Relationships

The substitution of chord forms from the parallel minor or major is a time-honored custom in tonal harmony. Altered chords commonly used in major, such as the diminished seventh chord on the leading tone, are borrowed from minor. In minor keys the major dominant is standard, and the Picardy (major) third in cadential tonics is an enduring convention. A contemporary usage of alternating minor and major tonic triads is shown in Example 154.

Ex. 154 BRITTEN: *A Ceremony of Carols, No. 4b* (1942)

If the principle of mode change is extended to embrace harmonies on all scale degrees and in all modes, each structure becomes available on every scale degree through substitution of mode without becoming subject to the restrictions implicit in chromatic alteration. A glance at the table of modal triads in this chapter will confirm that all three triad qualities—major, minor, and diminished—occur on every degree of the scale in one or more of the modes.

The progressions of Example 155 do not yield to conventional analysis, but they are readily accounted for by the change of mode theory. Because of its prominence as a pedal tone in the bass, A is somewhat arbitrarily taken as the tonic for purposes of chord and mode identification.

Ex. 155 KHACHATURIAN: *Violin Concerto* (1940) p5

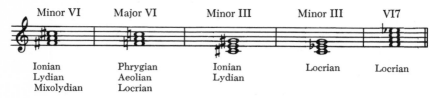

In his book *The Diatonic Modes in Modern Music* (University of California Press, 1951) John Vincent explores in detail change of mode with reference to triads and seventh chords. Obviously the principle can also be applied to other chord structures. Though the freedoms afforded by interchanging the modes are exercised extensively, there is no necessity in practice to classify chords according to their derivation. The following examples illustrate how contemporary composers have exploited free quality relationships between simple chord structures. The same procedures and relationships are equally feasible with complex chord formations.

The final cadence in the *Lament for Beowulf* consists of parallel, root position triads from different modes. In modern practice there are no taboos against cross (false) relations like those between the F minor and D major triads. On the contrary, cross relations are often featured in passages involving free quality relationships.

113

Ex. 156 HANSON: *Lament for Beowulf* (1925) p44

Cho.

D-flat and E-flat major triads are interposed between F major triads in Example 157, which has both contrary and parallel motion.

Ex. 157 STRAVINSKY: *Symphony of Psalms* (1930) p46

The following is another example of major triads with contrary motion between the outer parts in three of the four progressions. The root relationships—down a minor second, up a diminished third, down a minor third, and up a major second to the initial chord—are as interesting as they are unusual.

Ex. 158 BRITTEN: *Serenade—Sonnet* (1943)

In the next example four minor triads are followed by two major triads. The interval between the chord roots—a major third, a tritone, a perfect fourth, a major second, and a minor third—is different in each progression.

Ex. 159 HARRIS: *American Ballads, No. 1* (1947)

Free chord quality relationships are strikingly illustrated in the concluding section of *Mathis der Maler*. Some of the octave doublings have been omitted in the example and the pitches have been transposed up a semitone from the original to facilitate reading and playing on the piano. It is noteworthy that this thoroughly modern work ends with seventeen measures in which there are only major and minor triads, two seventh chords, and one nonchord tone. These simple harmonies produce a powerful effect when they are played triple forte by the full brass choir as scored.

Ex. 160 HINDEMITH: *Mathis der Maler* (1934) p89

The free interchange of modal chord qualities and de-emphasis of fourth and fifth root movements leads inevitably to a relaxation of tonal influence on harmonic relationships and a more contemporary idiom. In the commentary relating to the following examples only root movements are mentioned, but the qualities of the chords built on the roots and the nonfunctional nature of the progressions are also factors in the style of the excerpts, which is uncomplicated but modern.

Approaching the final cadence in the first movement of *Mathis der Maler*, Hindemith uses root movements in seconds in lieu of a traditional cadence formula. A pedal tone on the fifth degree of the scale is sustained while the moving parts expand. Chord roots, which in this instance coincide with the bass, are shown on a separate staff directly beneath the chords.

Ex. 161 HINDEMITH: *Mathis der Maler* (1934) p32

Example 162 begins with major triads on roots descending stepwise. The root, third, and fifth of the triads in turn are in the bass, producing an ascending bass line in contrary motion with the soprano. The ascending minor second root progression at the end sounds like a deceptive cadence in B minor.

Ex. 162 PROKOFIEV: *Classical Symphony in D* (1917) p41

The root movements are varied in Example 163. The perfect fifth (fourth), tritone, ascending minor third, descending major third, descending major second, and ascending major second are represented in its five measures.

Ex. 163 BARTOK: *Piano Concerto No. 3* (1945) p32

The beginning of the melody in Example 164 is a mirror inversion of that in Example 163. In this setting the intervals between roots are thirds and perfect fifths alternately until the final tritone progression.

Ex. 164 BARTOK: *Piano Concerto No. 3* (1945) p32

Parallelism

Consecutive thirds, sixths, octaves, and first inversion triads were permitted during the common practice period, but parallelism involving other intervals and chord forms was studiously avoided until the advent of impressionism. Pioneered by Debussy and Ravel, parallelism has virtually become their hallmark. In the first part of the century it played a vital role in the liberation of voice leading and in the emergence of new concepts of tonal organization. Parallel motion tends to reduce the functional value of chords and to emphasize the coloristic aspect of harmony.

Parallelism can be implemented in several ways. One of the simplest is illustrated in Example 165 where the melody is doubled in octaves, and the octaves are filled in to form root position triads. The effect of these same chords connected in accordance with traditional principles would be quite different. Major and minor triad qualities are used, but diminished and augmented are avoided, making all of the fourths and fifths perfect.

Ex. 165 DEBUSSY: *Piano Preludes, Book II No. 10—Canope* (1913)

Ravel uses parallel triads with emphasis on the major quality to accompany an independent melody in his *Piano Sonatine.*

Ex. 166 RAVEL: *Piano Sonatine* (1905) p2

Parallelism is not a device of impressionism or triads exclusively. Stravinsky uses it with first inversion seventh chords with the fifth omitted and then with complete seventh chords in root position. All of the notes are in D-flat major, so every diatonic seventh chord is heard in the scale-wise progressions.

Ex. 167 STRAVINSKY: *Firebird Suite* (1910) p40

In the next two examples parallel motion between ninth chords is illustrated. All of the ninth chords have the root in the bass and the ninth in the soprano, which is the most usual arrangement.

Ex. 168 DEBUSSY: *Pelleas and Melisande* (1902) p14

Ex. 169 DEBUSSY: *Nocturnes—Fêtes* (1899)

Stravinsky's use of parallel ninth chords in *Petrouchka* is similar to but more varied than his use of parallel seventh chords shown in Example 167.

Ex. 170 STRAVINSKY: *Petrouchka* (1911) p52

In Example 171 the chords in the bass clef are major triads in the second inversion ascending stepwise. The F and G in the treble clef are added sixths. The C in the third measure can be analyzed as an added second, as a pedal tone, or as a suspension which resolves down to the B-flat in the next measure.

Ex. 171 HINDEMITH: *Mathis der Maler* (1934) p62

Parallelism is not a feature of Schoenberg's style, but Example 172 is one instance where he used parallel seventh chords. This example demonstrates that the device can be adapted to diverse styles and that it can appear in more subtle forms than block chords moving in uniform rhythms. The right-hand part is rhythmically and harmonically independent. The left-hand part outlines root position seventh chords in a pattern that shifts in relation to the meter.

Ex. 172 SCHOENBERG: *Three Piano Pieces, Op. 11 No. 2* (1910)

In the first part of the century parallelism was a fresh, new device for which composers found many uses, and numerous works employing it endure as staple concert fare. Emphasis in more recent times has shifted away from the type of harmonic thinking that led to parallelism, and now it has little appeal for serious composers. Parallel motion is prevalent, however, in the current pop and rock music.

The harmonic resources of the common practice period considered as isolated chord structures and individual root movements can be summed up in a page or two, but extensive courses in traditional harmony are devoted to a systematic study of these limited materials. An equally exhaustive investigation of contemporary harmony would require volumes and years, but such thoroughness is impractical and unwarranted. The foregoing introduction to early twentieth-century harmonic practices provides an adequate foundation for exploring subsequent developments. Additional analysis and synthesis is recommended to improve one's understanding of and skill in handling new harmonic resources. Composers instinctively adopt materials and methods compatible with their musical ideas, and their personal styles emerge as ideas and resources are fused into a unified creative expression.

Suggested Assignments

1. Locate examples of modal harmony in twentieth-century music. Identify the modes and describe their influence on the chord qualities and relationships.

2. Write appropriate modal settings for the modal melodies composed previously.
3. Determine the tonal centers and do a chord and mode analysis of Examples 156, 157, 158, and 160 using the format of Example 155 as a model.
4. Compare the chord root relationships in Examples 148 and 149 with those customary in tonal music.
5. Analyze the root relationships in the third movement of Prokofiev's *Classical Symphony.*
6. Provide accompaniments featuring free quality and root relationships for original or assigned melodies.
7. Locate and analyze examples of parallelism in Debussy's *Piano Preludes.*
8. Write an exercise in which parallel progressions predominate.
9. Starting from the isolated chord structures written as assignments for Chapter 6, write effective resolutions and/or progressions of three or four chords. Strive for a consistent, homogeneous effect within each progression and for variety between progressions.
10. For supplementary reading see *Twentieth-Century Harmony* by Vincent Persichetti (W. W. Norton, 1961) and *Contemporary Harmony* by Ludmila Ulehla (The Free Press, 1966).

8

Tonality

$\mathcal{W}$HEN tones are sounded in orderly melodic successions or harmonic progressions, tonality ordinarily results. The tendency for one tone to emerge as the center of sound complexes is a phenomenon observable in music from a wide range of periods and styles. Only when consciously avoided is this tendency absent, but it exists in many degrees. In straightforward major and minor keys tonality is the basis for the strong functional relationships, and it exerts a decisive influence on every phrase and progression. The bonds of conventional key feeling are weakened by the use of modes, exotic and synthetic scales, dissonant harmonies, free quality and root relationships, and parallel motion, but a tonal center is usually discernible at cadence points and critical junctures in the form in all but deliberately atonal music. As long as tonal centers serve as focal points no matter how indecisively and can be perceived no matter how fleetingly, the music has tonality in the broad and inclusive sense of the term intended in this chapter. One distinct advantage of preserving some vestige of tonality is that without it, modulation is impossible.

Modulation and Transposition

Tonality is a prime source of both variety and unity in all music which has it. Modulating from one tonality to another provides variety; returning to the original tonality provides unity. Before the acceptance of equal temperament and the perfection of valves, compositions for many instruments were restricted by practical considerations to a small group of related keys. Even when remote keys became accessible, their full potential was not exploited immediately. It remained for contemporary composers, unhampered by mechanical imperfections or conventions, to explore routinely the far corners of the tonal universe. In twentieth-century styles no tonality is too remote to be reached by direct modulation within or between phrases or to be used in the transposition of themes in the larger forms.

Hindemith, whose music is frankly tonal, uses modulations and transpositions to foreign keys with consummate skill, and almost any page of his scores will provide examples. Those in *Mathis der Maler* are typical. The following excerpt from the beginning of the second movement starts in C. The cadence at the end of the first phrase is on G-sharp. The first chord of the second phrase is G-sharp minor, though some notes are spelled enharmonically as shown in the reduction. This two-measure phrase leads back to the opening motive at the original pitch but with octave doublings and shifted from the first beat of the measure to the third. The end of the phrase is changed to cadence this time on a C-sharp minor chord, which is also the beginning of a contrasting transitional passage. Within the first ten measures of the movement there are transient modulations from C to G-sharp, back to C, and then to C-sharp.

Ex. 173 HINDEMITH: *Mathis der Maler* (1934) p33

The tonal relationships of the theme are characteristic of the movement as a whole. When the theme given above returns to complete a ternary form, it begins a step lower in B-flat and ends in F-sharp major. The movement which starts in C concludes, after a coda, in C-sharp major.

Similar remote tonal relationships are exhibited in the first movement of this same work. The design is that of sonata form except that the order of the subordinate and closing themes is reversed in the recapitulation, and the key relationships are atypical. The beginnings of the principal, subordinate, and closing themes are shown in Example 174, first as they appear in the exposition and then as they reappear in the recapitulation. The principal and subordinate themes are both a semitone higher in the recapitulation. The closing theme is a major third lower.

Ex. 174 HINDEMITH: *Mathis der Maler* (1934)

The first movement of *Mathis der Maler* begins and ends with G as the tonal center. The final cadence is shown in Example 161. The statement of the principal theme, after an introduction, begins over G harmony. Its return in the recapitulation a semitone higher is accompanied by a D-flat major chord, with the D-flat spelled enharmonically as C-sharp. Beginning the recapitulation in a remote key violates a cardinal rule of classic form, but it is quite acceptable by contemporary standards. Reversing the order of the subordinate and closing themes in the recapitulation brings the subordinate theme back near the end of the movement, and transposing it up a semitone brings it back in the key of the movement to complete a perfectly rational tonal design.

The final movement proper of *Mathis der Maler* begins, after a tonally ambiguous introduction, in C-sharp minor. This movement concludes with the passage quoted a semitone higher than actual pitch as Example 160. The final chord, D-flat major, can be explained as the parallel major of C-sharp minor written enharmonically. This parallel relationship is more nearly conventional than the tritone relationship between the first and last movements, the former having G as the tonal center and the latter C-sharp and D-flat. It should be mentioned that the music was conceived originally as part of an opera, not as a symphony, and that the hymn tune *Es sungen drei Engel* is quoted in D-flat in the introduction and again in the development section of the first movement.

These examples from Hindemith illustrate typical explorations of remote tonalities in twentieth-century music. It is obvious that the relationships which were shunned by composers in the past have had special appeal for the tonal composers of this century.

Shifting Tonality

Abrupt change of tonality is a mannerism of certain Soviet composers which has sufficient currency to justify its consideration. Related to modulation in traditional music, shifting tonality contrasts with conventional modulation in three basic respects. Where conventional modulations are prepared with common material and proceed smoothly to a related key, contemporary shifts in tonality are unprepared and move precipitately to a remote tonal region. These procedures are foreshadowed somewhat in the free quality relationships of chords, but free quality relationships may orbit a single tonal center. Shifting tonality implies a sudden displacement of the old center by a new one. Since the surprise element is crucial, the device is most effective when the harmonic materials are unsophisticated and both tonalities are fairly obvious. As a rule the new key appears unexpectedly at a strategic point in the phrase structure.

The unanticipated tonal shifts in Example 175 are from D to A-flat and then to G.

Ex. 175 PROKOFIEV: *Classical Symphony in D* (1917) p49

Example 176 has a similar shift of tonality but returns to the original center at the end.

Ex. 176 PROKOFIEV: *Peter and the Wolf* (1936) p1

Stgs.

Shostakovich is another Soviet composer in whose music examples of shifting tonality abound. The following, taken from his *Fifth Symphony*, has some chromatic notes before the actual shifts, but the effect is only slightly diminished.

Ex. 177 SHOSTAKOVICH: *Symphony No. 5* (1937)

a. p58

b. p66

Tonal shifts, used judiciously, are an effective adjunct to compositional resources. Used excessively, they become an annoying mannerism.

Dual Modality

The possibility of using successive chords from different modes with the same tonal center was explored in the preceding chapter. When material from two modes is used simultaneously, the result is *dual modality*. The special quality of dual modality is most apparent when two inflections of the same note occur together or in close proximity. Though theoretically possible with the ecclesiastical modes, dual modality is common only between major and minor.

Oscillation between major and minor thirds in sustained chords is a characteristic feature of Example 178, where it occurs in five of the nine measures. The minor third of the D-flat chord in measure 4 is spelled enharmonically, as is the minor seventh. The chord on the second beat of measure 2 contains both E and E-flat, but its sound is that of an E seventh chord with a major third spelled enharmonically as A-flat and a major seventh spelled enharmonically as E-flat.

Ex. 178 HARRIS: *Symphony No. 3* (1938) p4

In Example 179 dual modality produces consistent cross relations between sonorities containing either B-flat or B-natural.

Ex. 179 COPLAND: *Piano Sonata* (1941) p5

Example 180, with a melody entirely in A minor and an accompaniment essentially in A major, effectively illustrates dual modality between melody and harmony.

Ex. 180 BARTOK: *String Quartet No. 2* (1917) p17

A more extended and systematic use of dual modality is illustrated in Example 181. From the beginning to the first cadence the upper part is drawn exclusively from C minor, the lower part from C major. The modes of the two parts are reversed during the next six measures, after which each part returns to its original mode.

Ex. 181 BARTOK: *Mikrokosmos, No. 59—Major and Minor* (1926–37)

Elements of A major and A minor are distributed between the two hands in the dance for piano from which Example 182 is taken. The conflicting notes in the two modes occur both simultaneously and in succession.

Ex. 182 MILHAUD: *Saudades do Brazil, No. 8—Tijuca* (1921)

Dual modality is a specialized effect with limited applications, but one capable of providing delightfully pungent sounds with resources not far removed from the familiar major and minor.

Polytonality

It is but a short step from the use of two modes to the use of two tonalities. This is known as *polytonality*. Strictly speaking, *bitonality* would be a more accurate designation, since more than two tonal centers at the same time are rare, but polytonality is the more prevalent term. Revolutionary as the idea of polytonality may seem, it is not unprecedented. Incipient polytonality can be detected in strongly tonal music. For example, the answer and countersubject in the exposition of a real fugue may suggest different keys briefly when played separately even though they are perceived as being in the same key when played together. The countersubject by itself may continue to imply the tonic key (of the subject) until distinctive material of the new key such as its leading tone is introduced. The answer enters meanwhile directly in the dominant key. This is not conceived as a polytonal effect. It results spontaneously from the preponderance of common tones between the two keys. In contrast with this are the calculated exploitations of remote polytonal relationships in modern music.

Dissonant harmony and counterpoint frequently have polytonal implications, but the term is usually reserved for passages in which two or more tonal centers are rather clearly apparent. In this respect it should be noted that they often are more obvious to the eye than to the ear. Listeners are perfectly capable of appreciating the effect even when they are not able to isolate the two keynotes. For polytonality to be consciously perceived, the two keys must be relatively pure and adequately separated in register or timbre.

Milhaud was an early exponent of polytonality, and it can be detected in many of his works. The following example illustrates polytonality, and also dual modality to which it is related. The accompaniment outlines tonic and dominant seventh chords in G major while the melody is in D major for the first eight measures. Then the melody shifts abruptly to G minor while the accompaniment continues its pattern in G major.

Ex. 183 MILHAUD: *Saudades do Brazil, No. 7—Corcovado* (1921)

The polytonality in Britten's setting of *The Ash Grove* is particularly interesting because of the key change in the counterpoint on the repetition of the melody. Against the folk song in F, the added part is first in B-flat and then in D-flat, except for the one G-natural.

Ex. 184 BRITTEN: *Folk Songs of the British Isles, Vol. I No. 6* (1943)

The black key-white key polytonality shown in Example 185 is a favorite in music for piano.

Ex. 185 MILHAUD: *Violin Sonata No. 2* (1917) p14

In Example 186 strict canonic imitation at the interval of a minor ninth produces dissonant polytonal polyphony. The mode is pure Dorian on D and C-sharp. The note heads are reproduced in two sizes as they appear in the original notation.

Ex. 186 HOVHANESS: *Allegro on a Pakistan Lute Tune* (1952)

In the foregoing examples each tonality was founded on a major, minor, or modal scale, but other scales can figure in polytonal textures. Example 187 is based on the two whole-tone scales used in a manner which produces constant melodic doubling in minor thirds. This, like any uniform interval doubling, has polytonal implications (see Chapter 4).

Polytonality can be used in both contrapuntal and homophonic styles and between closely related and remote keys to produce many degrees of dissonance and complexity. Drawing material from two recognizable tonalities simultaneously is another way concepts of tonal organization have been expanded in the twentieth century.

Pandiatonicism

Pandiatonicism is a term coined by Nicolas Slonimsky to describe music which, in reaction to excessive tonal chromaticism and atonality, reverts to the resources of the diatonic scale. Only the absence of characteristic melodic and harmonic functions sets it apart from conventional diatonic music, so pandiatonicism is used sparingly by contemporary composers. Traditional chord progressions, melodic patterns, and cadence formulas are avoided to preserve a somewhat modern, if quaint, flavor. The following pandiatonic passage is typical.

Ex. 187 COPLAND: *Appalachian Spring* (1944) p51

In this chapter ways of adapting tonality to contemporary requirements have been explored. The alternatives are simply to abandon tonality or to substitute something else in its place, possibilities examined in Chapter 14.

Suggested Assignments

1. Locate and describe a twentieth-century example of each of the following:
   a. Modulation or transposition to a remote key
   b. Shifting tonality
   c. Dual modality
   d. Polytonality
   e. Pandiatonicism
2. Write a concise original exercise which modulates or shifts to a remote tonality.
3. Compose a minor melody with an accompaniment in the parallel major key.
4. Write a polytonal two-part counterpoint exercise.
5. Write a passage for piano featuring black key-white key polytonality.
6. Compose a short piece which is at least partially pandiatonic.
7. For additional reading on tonality see Rudolf Reti's *Tonality in Modern Music* (Collier Books, 1962).

9

Cadences

SINCE cadences in the periods preceding our own were constructed from a limited number of stereotyped formulas, expansion of the cadence concept in the present century was inevitable. However, certain considerations peculiar to cadence points restrain the renunciation of traditional patterns. Listeners thoroughly conditioned to perfect authentic cadences are disturbed by radical departures from their preconceived configurations. Furthermore, the dissonant harmonies which dominate contemporary music and serve admirably in building tension within phrases are deficient in the repose quality required to conclude them. For these reasons cadences in contemporary idioms pose special problems. Composers in their quest for fresh cadential materials seek tonal combinations which will be perceived as cadences, because the aural perception of cadences is essential to the comprehension of music, especially in matters of form.

Representative contemporary cadence procedures are illustrated. For the sake of uniformity the examples have been selected from final cadences ending works or movements, but the same types are found within movements providing both complete and incomplete cadence functions. The distinctions between complete and incomplete cadences formerly made on the basis of chord structures and progressions are no longer valid. Cadential resources are too varied to be classified on that basis, but they do not introduce chord structures or progressions that have not been studied previously. Rather, they show these materials serving cadential functions. Since cadences are completely meaningful only in connection with the entire musical idea they bring to a close, the passages preceding the examples should be examined whenever possible.

Modified Dominants

In conventional music the formula for a complete cadence ordinarily consists of a progression from dominant to tonic. Not only does the dominant have a specified structure and stand in a fixed relationship to the tonic, but the movement of the individual voices is regulated by tradition. The only facet of this formula honored consistently by contemporary composers is the progression of an active sound to a less active or repose sound, and even this has its exceptions. The contemporary cadences, which have most in common with convention are those which keep the dominant-tonic function intact and modify only the structure of the dominant and/or its relationship to the tonic.

Example 188 has the traditional fifth relationship between the dominant and tonic and differs from tradition only in the use of the minor dominant and the upward resolution of its seventh. The diverging chromatic lines contribute to the cadential effect. The D-sharp and F-natural in the chromatic lines are heard as chromatic passing tones against the D-natural and F-sharp of the chord.

Ex. 188 BARTOK: *Piano Concerto No. 3* (1945) p91

The fifth relationship is preserved, but the structure of the dominant in Example 189 represents a further departure from convention.

139

Ex. 189 BARTOK: *Concerto for Orchestra* (1943) p28

The interval of a perfect fifth on the leading tone provides the dominant function in Example 190.

Ex. 190 HARRIS: *Symphony No. 3* (1938) p103

The final chord of Example 191 is preceded by a sonority which sounds like a D7 chord with an unresolved 4–3 suspension. Because of the G-naturals in the imitation just before, the G-sharp in the cadence chord has a Picardy third effect.

Ex. 191 BARTOK: *Piano Concerto No. 3* (1945) p48

Typical dominant function is missing in Example 192 where the passing D's and the A-flat minor triad come between the major tonic triad and the final tonic note, F.

Ex. 192 SHOSTAKOVICH: *Symphony No. 1* (1925) p92

Modified Tonics

Notes can be added to cadential tonic triads without distorting them beyond recognition. In Example 193 the C tonic with an added sixth is approached from an inverted B minor seventh chord.

Ex. 193 STRAVINSKY: *Histoire du Soldat* (1918) p6

The final chord of Stravinsky's *Symphony in Three Movements* has an added sixth and an added second.

140

Ex. 194 STRAVINSKY: *Symphony in Three Movements* (1945) p120

All of the notes of the tonic and dominant triads in C major are combined in the final chord of Prokofiev's *Third Piano Concerto.*

Ex. 195 PROKOFIEV: *Piano Concerto No. 3* (1921) p180

In Example 196 dual modality is carried over to the concluding tonic, which has both major and minor thirds.

Ex. 196 BARTOK: *Mikrokosmos, No. 108—Wrestling* (1926–37)

The net effect of *The Rite of Spring*'s final sonority, with its dissonant elements and close spacing in a low register, is percussive. Neither this chord nor the way it is approached bears any resemblance to a traditional cadence, but they serve the purpose admirably in this particular work.

Ex. 197 STRAVINSKY: *The Rite of Spring* (1913) p139

The next step after using a percussive sonority for a cadential tonic is using unaccompanied percussion instruments to make a cadence, as Stravinsky does in the following example.

Ex. 198 STRAVINSKY: *Histoire du Soldat* (1918) p68

Linear Cadences

The motion of the individual voices is always of primary importance at cadence points. Linear motion is more decisive in some cadences than harmonic progression. This is necessarily the case when a composition ends like *Petrouchka* with a single line. The dominant-tonic relationship is established between the C-sharps and F-sharps in spite of the intervening D-sharps and C-naturals.

142

Ex. 199 STRAVINSKY: *Petrouchka* (1911) p171

The diverging lines of Example 200 are reminiscent of those in Example 188, and they expand to an octave as did the outer parts in many prebaroque cadences. The stepwise approach to the tonic note with two voices in contrary motion is a venerable cadence device.

Ex. 200 BARTOK: *String Quartet No. 5* (1934) p92

The outer parts in Example 201 expand by step to an open fifth, C-G. The penultimate chord, a D-flat major triad, is the Neapolitan chord in the key of C. Neapolitan chords traditionally are used in the first inversion preceding the dominant in cadence progressions. Only in more recent times have they been used in root position as dominant substitutes, a function illustrated in the following example. Though the key of the fugue is A-flat as indicated in the title, it ends (atypically for this work) on C.

Ex. 201 HINDEMITH: *Ludus Tonalis—Fuga Septima in A-flat* (1943)

Noncadential Endings

Some compositions end without any approximation or reasonable facsimile of a traditional cadence.The active-repose elements or strong linear motion long considered essential are lacking. Endings of this sort—the word cadence hardly seems appropriate—are associated with atonal and, more particularly, twelve-tone music like the next two examples from Schoenberg. The last two measures of his *Fourth String Quartet* contain all twelve notes in an order derived from the series on which the quartet is based. Five of them are still sounding at the end.

Ex. 202 SCHOENBERG: *String Quartet No. 4* (1936) p107

The solo part in the following ending suggests B-flat as the tonal center, but this tonality is not substantiated in the other parts. As in the preceding example all twelve notes appear, and this time eight of them are sustained in the fermata which ends the movement.

144

Ex. 203 SCHOENBERG: *Violin Concerto* (1936) p28

In noncadential endings and cadences which tend to be ambiguous, tempo and dynamics assume added importance. Cadences which otherwise might be unconvincing are made believable by ritardandos, diminuendos, fermatas, and the like. Repetition also helps to establish cadential function. Observe the repetition in the top part of both Schoenberg examples. Harmonic progression, melodic line, rhythm, tempo, and (in performance) phrasing are factors capable of contributing to the cadential effect. When some of these elements are obscure or missing, the others must compensate for cadences to be successful. Interpretation is especially important at internal cadence points in unfamiliar idioms.

In contemporary composition it is neither possible nor desirable to adhere to ready-made cadence formulas. A suitable cadence—one appropriate to the style and medium and fulfilling the structural requirements—is devised for each cadence point in modern works. This makes composition, performance, and perception more difficult, but also more interesting and challenging.

Suggested Assignments

1. Analyze several final cadences in contemporary compositions and classify them according to the headings in this chapter.
2. Examine the cadences in your previous composition exercises and change any that can be improved using the devices introduced in this chapter.
3. Write a short exercise ending with a cadence having a modified dominant and/or tonic.
4. Compose some phrases for two melodic instruments which end with modern, linear cadences.

10

Nonharmonic Materials

$\mathcal{W}$HEN the harmony consists of triads and seventh chords exclusively, isolating the nonharmonic material is a simple process. Any tone which does not belong to a recognized chord is a nonchord or nonharmonic tone by definition. Nonharmonic tones in this context are classified according to the way they are approached and left, their relationship to the prevailing harmony, and their position relative to the beats and accents. Harmony texts deal exhaustively with the types of nonharmonic tones found in traditional music and with the restrictions customarily observed by the composers of the common practice period. Formerly, nonharmonic tones moved by step between chord tones or resolved by step to chord tones with few exceptions. The designations and definitions are not completely standardized, but common descriptive names are: *passing tones, neighboring* or *auxiliary tones, suspensions, anticipations, escape tones* or *échappées, appoggiaturas, changing tones* or *cambiatas,* and *pedal points.*

By whatever name they are known, all of the melodic patterns and relationships in the conventional nonharmonic classifications remain viable, but the sharp dividing line between harmonic and nonharmonic has disappeared along with the restrictions. No clear distinction is possible when every conceivable dissonance is permissible within the harmony. Notes are perceived as being nonharmonic in modern music only when their resemblance to one of the familiar categories is obvious or the harmonies are relatively uncomplicated. Many sounds which otherwise would have been unacceptable in conventional music were allowed as nonharmonic tones, but such justifications for dissonances are no longer required. In this survey of nonharmonic materials in twentieth-century music, no attempt has been made to recapitulate those practices covered in traditional theory or those which represent only slight modifications. Those considered are intended to reflect the more relaxed attitude regarding the treatment of dissonance in the music of our time.

One manifestation of this attitude is in the freedom with which dissonances are left by leap. The B-flats in Example 204 are left by leap in both directions, though they are dissonant with the prevailing D minor harmony. Because of their short duration and unaccented position in the measures, they are heard as nonharmonic tones, not as roots of a B-flat major seventh chord.

Ex. 204 WALTON: *Belshazzar's Feast* (1931) p2

Against the more complex harmonic background in Example 205 dissonant melody tones are left by leap with equal freedom. The melodic line, which at first glance seems to consist of random pitches, actually has an intricate design. Each fragment is immediately mirrored, though the intervals are not exact, while the notes on the beat descend chromatically for a full octave. The bass moves up chromatically, complementing the descending motion of the melody.

Ex. 205 BARTOK: *Mikrokosmos, No. 147—March* (1926–37)

Passing tones, too, are treated with added freedom in this century. Example 206 has a scale in sixths combined with seventh chord progressions. In the scale line there are chord tones and single and double passing tones. When a passing tone fills an interval between chord tones, a cluster results. Unlike conventional passing tones, which most often come between chord changes and are of shorter duration than the chords with which they are associated, these passing tones move with the chords.

Ex. 206 STRAVINSKY: *Firebird Suite* (1910) p77

Conventional passing tones normally are unrepeated and move without interruption to chord tones. Example 207 has double passing tones which not only form clusters with chord tones and are reiterated but which are separated by rests from their resolutions.

Ex. 207 KODALY: *Te Deum* (1936) p26

The progressions in Example 208 are the direct descendants of conventional passing chords despite the relatively high level of dissonance and the lack of rhythmic independence. The voice leading, which is important, cannot be adequately conveyed in a condensation of the score.

Ex. 208 HINDEMITH: *Mathis der Maler* (1934) p7

Complete passing chords also occur in contemporary music while the prevailing harmony is sustained or repeated, as in Example 209.

Ex. 209 STRAVINSKY: *Petrouchka* (1911) p39

The middle line of Example 210 has double and triple counterparts of unprepared chromatic lower neighboring tones.

Ex. 210 PISTON: *Divertimento* (1946) p10

The effect of Example 211 is like that of triple neighboring tones, though not all of them resolve stepwise. It is also reminiscent of white key-black key polytonality.

Ex. 211 HINDEMITH: *Ludus Tonalis—Interludium* (1943) p38

The structure of an unresolved 4–3 suspension on various pitches persists without interruption for the duration of a short piano piece by William Schuman. The beginning and the end, with the eventual resolution, are shown in Example 212.

Ex. 212 SCHUMAN: *Three-Score Set, No. 1* (1943)

Pedal points and ostinato figures usually begin and end consonantly in conventional music but not necessarily in contemporary styles. The tonality shift in the upper voices is not reflected in the bass of Example 213.

Ex. 213 SHOSTAKOVICH: *Symphony No. 9* (1945) p8

The pedal D in Example 214 is introduced as a consonance but is left momentarily after a dissonance. The harmonies above it range further afield than would be possible in earlier styles to give the excerpt a thoroughly modern flavor.

Ex. 214 WALTON: *Belshazzar's Feast* (1931) p3

The pedal point in the top voice of Example 215 is introduced and left as a dissonance and is in a remote relationship to the sonorities under it.

Ex. 215 HINDEMITH: *Mathis der Maler* (1934) p37

Pedal points can be double (consist of two notes) and rhythmic as well as single and sustained. Example 216 shows a double pedal point with a vigorous two-measure rhythmic pattern which persists unchanged for twenty-eight measures near the beginning of Walton's *First Symphony*. Other notes take the place of the F after that, but the B-flats and the rhythm are retained for thirty-nine additional measures.

Ex. 216 WALTON: *Symphony No. 1* (1935) p1

Repeated patterns of more than two notes are considered as ostinatos in Chapter 11.

The foregoing examples suffice to demonstrate that contemporary composers, though completely emancipated in their treatment of dissonances, still have found many uses for musical materials with a recognizable relationship to the traditional categories of nonharmonic tones.

Suggested Assignments

1. Find examples of nonharmonic tones in contemporary music. Analyze and classify them.
2. Review exercises written for previous assignments to see if any of them can be improved by adding nonharmonic tones.
3. Write an exercise with a relatively simple harmonic background and a melody which has dissonances approached and left by leap.
4. Employ passing tones or passing chords in an unconventional manner in an original exercise.
5. Write an effective harmonic progression over or under a pedal point.
6. Write a two-part exercise in which dissonances between the voices are resolved in an unconventional manner.

11

Motivation of Harmony

I N homophonic music various means of sustaining the sound of chords and motivating them rhythmically are necessary. These requirements were satisfied during the classic and romantic periods by repeated chords and sundry arpeggio figurations, including Alberti bass. Basic types of harmonic motivation were modified and embellished for variety, and contrapuntal procedures were always available to relieve the monotony of a strictly homophonic style. The search for new ways to motivate harmony seems not to have been a primary concern in past centuries, but in this one composers have been reluctant to employ stereotyped formulas in harmonic motivation as in any other function. This reluctance is partially responsible no doubt for the fact that contemporary composers on the whole have been less prolific than their predecessors. The pursuit of total originality is a time-consuming and sometimes unrewarding occupation, so vestiges of the old accompaniment patterns persist. Creative imagination functions in adapting and applying them to twentieth-century sonorities, progressions, and rhythms. The following examples illustrate some of the possibilities.

Motivating New Harmonic Resources

The application of old procedures to new harmonic resources provides a simple solution to the problem of harmonic motivation. Except that it does not outline triads, the accompaniment figure in Example 217 could have come right out of Haydn or Mozart. The harmonic implications and the relationships between the melody and the accompaniment place it well within the present century.

Ex. 217 SHOSTAKOVICH: *Piano Preludes, No. 9* (1933)

The accompaniment figure in Example 218 is an obvious descendant of Alberti bass. The arpeggiated fourth chords, alternately in root position and first inversion, contribute to the fresh sound as do the relationships between them.

Ex. 218 BARTOK: *Mikrokosmos, No. 125—Boating* (1926–37)

Copyright 1940 by Hawkes & Son (London), Ltd.; Renewed 1967. Reprinted by permission of Boosey & Hawkes, Inc.

Repeated chords with unconventional structures also serve in modern accompaniment figures.

Ex. 219 BARTOK: *Mikrokosmos, No. 146—Ostinato* (1926–37)

Copyright 1940 by Hawkes & Son (London), Ltd.; Renewed 1967. Reprinted by permission of Boosey & Hawkes, Inc.

The accompaniment in Example 220 can be analyzed either as an open fifth with neighboring tones or as a rapid alternation of fifths and thirds, but it will probably be heard as a rhythmically animated sonority consisting of all four notes—E, F-sharp, A, and B.

Ex. 220 BARTOK: *Piano Concerto No. 3* (1945) p1

The affinity between the accompaniment in Example 221 and some found in Brahms is apparent at a glance. A closer examination reveals the source of its distinctive contemporary flavor in the more complex chord outlines.

Ex. 221 PROKOFIEV: *Piano Concerto No. 3* (1921) p36

In Example 222, which illustrates a relatively new manner of motivating harmonic sound, it is possible to detect elements of imitation, inversion, and a polychord, but the total effect is that of an animated A major seventh chord.

Ex. 222 HARRIS: *Symphony No. 3* (1938) p23

The polychordal arpeggios in contrary motion, three notes against four, shown in Example 223 represent the greatest departure from conventional accompaniment figures yet illustrated.

Ex. 223 BLOCH: *Violin Sonata No. 1* (1920) p6

Harmonic Motivation in Contemporary Rhythms

Most of the rhythmic features of contemporary music discussed in Chapter 5 have applications in the motivation of harmonies. Example 224 illustrates the use of shifting accents with a repeated polychord which serves as a harmonic background for fragmentary melodic ideas. The chord is scored for strings with the accents, which occur irregularly, reinforced by horns.

Ex. 224 STRAVINSKY: *The Rite of Spring* (1913) p11

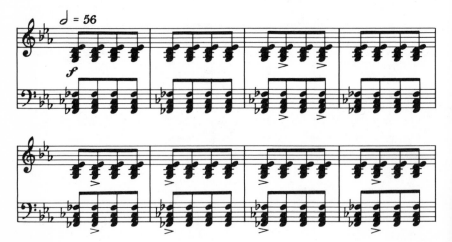

An asymmetric division of measures containing the equivalent of nine eighth notes is exploited in the accompaniment figure of Example 225.

Ex. 225 BARTOK: *Mikrokosmos, No. 148—Dance in Bulgarian Rhythm* (1926–37)

The accompaniment pattern shown in Example 226 reflects its asymmetric 5/4 meter.

Ex. 226 RAVEL: *Daphnis and Chloe, Suite No. 2* (1911) p76

Changing time signatures are basic to the harmonic motivation in the following example.

Ex. 227 COPLAND: *Appalachian Spring* (1944) p20

Accompaniment patterns, even comparatively mundane ones, gain freshness and vitality in the adaptations associated with contemporary rhythms.

Ostinato

Ostinato has undergone many transformations during the 700-plus years it has been a recognized musical procedure. That it has survived into the electronic age is ample proof of its viability. The following is a sampling of twentieth-century usages.

The first example is close to the baroque concept of ostinato—a constantly repeated bass line beneath changing upper parts. The C major scale pattern continues as an ostinato without interruption for thirty-three measures. Unusual by conventional standards is the 4½-measure length of the repeated line, which naturally does not coincide with the metric divisions.

Ex. 228 STRAVINSKY: *Octet* (1923) p32

More regular in length but less usual in line is the ostinato, derived from the introduction, which sounds throughout most of the coda to the third movement of *Mathis der Maler*.

Ex. 229 HINDEMITH: *Mathis der Maler* (1934) p83

The bass of Example 230 is a three-beat ostinato which shifts position in relation to the four-beat measures. The irregular spacing of the punctuating chords is independent of the ostinato figure, which continues for twenty-three measures. The time changes which occur throughout the passage are related to the upper parts, not the ostinato.

Ex. 230 STRAVINSKY: *Symphony in Three Movements* (1945) p8

A dissonant harmonic ostinato is illustrated in the next example. The rhythmically varied line on the top staff is for voice; the other four are in the orchestra. All five parts become an ostinato which continues as independent vocal lines enter in ensuing measures.

Ex. 231 MENOTTI: *The Medium* (1946) p23

An ostinato with imitation at the octave serves as accompaniment to a free melody in Example 232. The dotted bar lines in the imitating part are shown as they appear in the score.

Ex. 232 BARTOK: *String Quartet No. 5* (1934) p11

Example 233 has two pedal points, E and A, in addition to an ostinato with rhythmically varied imitation at the octave. This ostinato in the orchestra accompanies an independent vocal line.

Ex. 233 WALTON: *Belshazzar's Feast* (1931) p11

In the following example the ostinato in the bass clef draws its notes from F major, while the notes in the treble clef are from F-sharp major. Ostinatos provide a simple and effective means of creating polytonal effects.

Ex. 234 MILHAUD: *Piano Sonata* (1916) p3

The final ostinato example has two lines, both in eighth notes but moving independently. Of particular interest is the polytonal implication of the free voice in the work of a composer generally regarded as ultraconservative for his time. That the A/E-flat relationship is no mere coincidence is made clear by the subsequent statement of the same material with the tonalities reversed. The tritone is thematically significant in all four movements of this symphony. The ostinato is maintained essentially intact for ten measures in the first version and for eighteen in the second.

The same deviation from the pattern occurs just once in the upper part of both versions but not at the same point.

Ex. 235 SIBELIUS: *Symphony No. 4 in Am* (1911)

a. p42

b. p62

Methods of harmonic motivation cannot be divorced from the harmonies they articulate and the melodies they support. When melodic, harmonic, and rhythmic resources are richly varied as they are in twentieth-century music, accompaniment patterns are correspondingly endowed. Motivating devices facilitate composing by providing harmonic backgrounds with rhythmic interest while minimizing the problems of creating new patterns, new chords, and new lines. Since the motivating techniques come rather easily, composers are sometimes tempted to use them excessively.

Suggested Assignments

1. Find and analyze interesting examples of harmonic motivation in twentieth-century music for various mediums.
2. Motivate the block chord progressions given in Example 147 or some similar chord pattern in the following ways:
   a. In a pattern of three or four notes like an Alberti bass
   b. With irregularly spaced accents on repeated chords
   c. In arpeggio figures with more than an octave compass
   d. In an asymmetric meter
   e. With changing time signatures
   f. Over or under an ostinato
   It is not necessary to include every note of each chord in the motivated versions. Incomplete chords are common in rhythmically animated harmonic progressions.
3. Compose melodies to go with the more effective accompaniments devised for Assignment 2.
4. Write a short harmonic progression as an ostinato accompaniment to a rhythmically independent original melody.
5. Write a two-part ostinato which involves imitation.
6. Compose a melody and an ostinato accompaniment which together have polytonal implications.

12

Thematic Metamorphosis

*R*EPETITION is basic to the language of music. Meaningful music without repetition is almost inconceivable, and it is usually detectable even in the music of those few composers who strive to avoid it. For most composers it is not a question of eliminating repetition but of sustaining interest, which lags when literal repetition is excessive. Several procedures for modifying repetition which preserve its unifying values without placing interest in jeopardy are at the disposal of composers. The application of these procedures to thematic material produces the metamorphoses so characteristic of the compositional process.

Though exact reiteration has its place in music, modified repetition is more prevalent and useful. Nuances and instrumentation may vary in repetitions which otherwise are literal, but more significant changes involve pitch and rhythm. Such modifications applied to motives and themes sustain interest for extended periods with a minimum of source material. The exhaustive use of a few germ motives is highly conducive to essential unity. These facts have long been common knowledge, and the imaginative and skillful manipulation of thematic material is a continuing art, not an innovation. The processes of thematic transformation originated in the distant past, but their recent manifestations deserve attention.

Transposition and Sequence

The modification closest to exact repetition but still capable of providing variety is that of octave transposition. Though rhythm, line, and tonality remain the same, the theme is brought into the register of other instruments or shifted to a different register of the same instrument by octave transposition. This type of repetition has the advantage of being immediately apparent to the most casual listener without being utterly lacking in variety. Example 236 shows a melody with interesting contour and internal organization and its octave transposition. A study of these two excerpts in context substantiates the value of octave transposition in modified repetition.

Ex. 236 RAVEL: *Daphnis and Chloe, Suite No. 2* (1911)

a. p10

b. p19

Transposition by intervals other than the octave provides additional variety by implying either a different tonal center or a change of harmony, and intervallic relationships may be altered. Example 237 consists of a one-measure motive repeated sequentially, each time a third lower. The first and third measures have identical patterns, but the second has a minor third in place of a major third, an augmented fourth in place of one of the perfect fourths, and a diminished fifth in place of a perfect fifth.

Ex. 237 SIBELIUS: *Symphony No. 7 in C* (1924) p5

Interest is added to the sequential treatment of the motive in Example 238 by the slight rhythmic shift in the repetition and the change in relationship between the parts. The two upper voices are repeated sequentially a minor seventh higher with the top part doubled an octave below. The bass is also repeated sequentially, but a perfect fourth lower providing a fresh relationship. Even those who generally regard sequences as excessively repetitious would find little fault with this imaginative use of the device.

Ex. 238 PISTON: *Divertimento* (1946) p10

Systematic Modifications of Contour

Every musical line inherently has four basic forms: *original, inversion, retrograde,* and *retrograde inversion.* The inverted form presents the theme upside-down or as if seen in a mirror, going down where the original goes up and up where the original goes down. The retrograde form is like the original played backwards from the end to the beginning. Retrograde inversion is the retrograde form of the inversion or the original upside-down and backwards. All three of these modifications pose certain problems of perception to the listener, but they have persisted in the musical vocabulary for an extended period down to the present time. With but slight alteration all four forms of the theme —original, inversion, retrograde, and retrograde inversion—appear in the contemporary fugue from which Example 239 is taken.

Ex. 239 HINDEMITH: *Ludus Tonalis—Fuga Tertia in F* (1943)

Original

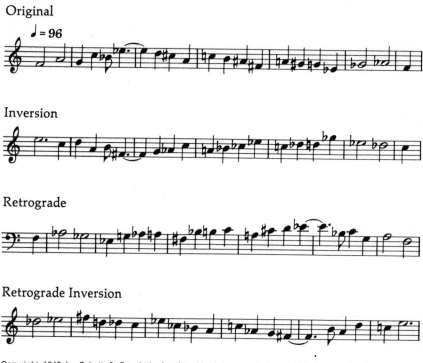

Inversion

Retrograde

Retrograde Inversion

The two retrograde forms are more difficult to perceive aurally than the inverted form in which the original rhythm is unaltered, and they are therefore less serviceable for purposes of unity. Most easily recognized and therefore most capable of contributing to unity is the inverted form which has a different version of the contour but the same rhythm as the original. The inversion can mirror the intervals of the original exactly or with some liberty, as in Example 240. The two forms of the theme appear consecutively starting in the measures indicated.

Ex. 240 BARTOK: *Mikrokosmos, No. 146—Ostinato* (1926–37)

a. m61

b. m68

The operation of the inversion principle is conspicuous in the two forms of the thematic fragment shown in Example 241, though the second version does not actually mirror the contour or duplicate the rhythm of the first.

Ex. 241 SHOSTAKOVICH: *Symphony No. 5* (1937)

a. p3

b. p45

Retrogrades are encountered less frequently than inversions in non-serial music, but they do occur. In Schoenberg's *Pierrot Lunaire, No. 18* the second half is an exact retrograde of the first half in the four upper parts. The *Postludium* in Hindemith's *Ludus Tonalis* is a literal retrograde inversion of the *Praeludium*. The parts are reversed from top to bottom so that even the location of the notes on, above, and below the staff is mirrored. Quoting these extended works is not feasible, but they are well worth studying.

Systematic Modifications of Rhythm

Inversion, retrograde, and retrograde inversion are systematic ways of modifying lines. *Augmentation* and *diminution* are systematic ways of modifying rhythms. Rhythmic values in augmentation are increased by a constant ratio, usually 1:2. Rhythmic values in diminution are reduced by a constant ratio, usually 2:1. For other ratios see Example 92. In reverse order, the original is the diminution of the augmentation and vice versa. The terms augmentation and diminution customarily refer to notation and not to tempo, which affects durations but not relative values.

Example 242 shows a theme in its original and augmented forms. The effect of the augmentation is somewhat counteracted by the faster tempo.

Ex. 242 SHOSTAKOVICH: *Symphony No. 5* (1937)

a. p109

b. p146

Example 243 also shows a theme in its original and augmented forms. In this case the purpose of the augmentation is to bring the theme back in the faster tempo sounding the same as it did originally.

Ex. 243 PROKOFIEV: *Piano Concerto No. 3* (1921)

a. p71

b. p108

A somewhat different type of rhythmic change is illustrated in Example 244. The material in each measure of the two versions corresponds, but the number of beats in a measure is reduced from three to two. At the same time, the metronome mark is reduced, but not sufficiently to make the two forms move at the same rate. Adjustments are made in the other values, but the three equal notes in a measure are preserved as a triplet.

Ex. 244 HINDEMITH: *Mathis der Maler* (1934)

a. p42

b. p77

Augmentation can be used within a theme, as it is in Example 245. The motive in the first measure returns with increased rhythmic values in the last three measures. The two forms of this motive enclose a contrasting motive and its varied repetition in a cogent theme.

Ex. 245 BARBER: *Symphony No. 1* (1936) p1

Within the space of seven score pages Shostakovich uses the same thematic motive in augmentation, in diminution, and in various transpositions.

172

Ex. 246 SHOSTAKOVICH: *Symphony No. 1* (1925)

a. p74

b. p78

c. p80

The preceding examples demonstrate that notating thematic elements in augmented and diminished values is used not only to double and halve durations but also to change the pace varying degrees and to preserve the original character in a different tempo.

Other Modifications

There are less systematic ways of transforming themes and motives which are not easily classified, and the systematic methods can be applied freely and in combinations. The passage quoted from *Appalachian Spring* illustrates some of the possibilities. It consists of nine consecutive versions of a single four-note motive. In the second version the value of the first two notes is reduced. The next version is a partial inversion. The fourth is a sequential repetition of the third a third lower and with the last note extended. The fifth appearance of the motive is an exact repetition of the second version. In the sixth and seventh versions the contour and rhythm of the third and fourth are repeated a perfect fourth higher.

The final version is a repetition of the preceding one with the last note extended one beat.

Ex. 247 COPLAND: *Appalachian Spring* (1944) p24

Roy Harris uses a different approach in the following thematic lines from his *Third Symphony*. Organic unity is sensed within each theme and between all three, but there is little actual repetition or obvious manipulation. This type of thematic transformation is conceived and perceived essentially by instinct, and no significant use is made of preconceived formulas. Though the unifying features do not yield readily to systematic analysis, they are apparent and effective.

Ex. 248 HARRIS: *Symphony No. 3* (1938)

a. p24

b. p25

c. p28

The opening motive of the Bartok *Second String Quartet* is altered continually as the movement progresses. The following are just a few of its many guises. Only the rhythm and the direction of the first three notes are constant. Other rhythmic values are lengthened and shortened; intervals are expanded and contracted; and linear motion is reversed; but the identity of the motive is never in doubt.

Ex. 249 BARTOK: *String Quartet No. 2* (1917)

More elaborate thematic metamorphosis occurs in Bartok's *Fourth Quartet*. Example 250 shows several versions of the motive which dominates both the first and last movements. Near the beginning it appears in its original form and immediately inverted (a). Some of the intervals and durations are expanded in the next version (b). A form of the motive with additional contour and rhythm modifications is stated in the low register and is answered immediately by its inversion in a higher octave (c). The remaining forms are from the last movement. In the first of these and its inversion the preceding pattern is shifted rhythmically and extended. The intervals and compass are expanded further, and the sixteenth notes are shifted back a half beat in the next version (f). Its essential features are preserved in a free inversion (g). The final melody (h), the last half of which is a free retrograde of the first half, is derived from the motive, but this inference is possible only by tracing it through the intervening transformations. Toward the end of the last movement the circle is completed, and the motive is heard again in its original form as it was at the beginning of the quartet.

Ex. 250 BARTOK: *String Quartet No. 4* (1928)

a. p4

b. p4

c. p8

d. p45

e. p46

f. p46

g. p47

h. p47

Peruse complete works at random for additional examples of the many and varied methods of thematic transformation. All of them will not be found in any one composition, but some of them will be. Thematic metamorphosis is basic in the construction of extended musical forms, and the ability to recognize thematic elements in all of their mutations is prerequisite to intelligent performing and listening.

Suggested Assignments

1. Locate examples of augmentation and diminution in twentieth-century music. Determine whether the changes in note values were made to alter the flow of the melodies or to preserve the original movement in a different tempo.
2. Catalog the transformation of the motives in Barber's *First Symphony* (see Example 245).
3. Find examples of thematic metamorphosis in the first and last movements of Bartok's *String Quartet No. 5.*
4. Write a motive and extend it by varied sequential repetition.
5. Compose a theme which is equally effective as nearly as possible in its original, inverted, retrograde, and inverted retrograde forms.
6. Write a theme in which a motive is used in augmentation and/or free inversion.
7. Construct an extended theme from a single concise motive by applying some of the procedures outlined in this chapter.
8. Write three different but similar melodies related in the manner of those in Example 248.
9. Create a motive and then write several modifications of it which could be used in a development section.
10. Compose a short piece based on a single motive and its transformations.
11. In *The Thematic Process in Music* by Rudolph Reti (Lawrence Verry, 1961) read the sections on Bartok's *Fourth String Quartet* and Debussy's *La Cathédrale Engloutie.*

13

Imitative Procedures

*T*HE practice of imitation dates back almost as far as the art of combining tones, but for centuries strictly observed conventions were formidable barriers to contrapuntal fluency. The ability to write imitation conforming to baroque and classic precepts was a notable achievement constituting somewhat of an end in itself, but this is not the case in modern styles. The permissiveness previously observed in connection with melodic invention and the treatment of dissonance applies equally to melodies in contrapuntal associations. Contrapuntal intricacy is no longer the evidence of technical mastery and the assurance of quality that it was before the obstacles which formerly thwarted novices were removed. The poet Robert Frost is quoted as saying that writing free verse is like playing tennis with the net down. The analogy might well be applied to writing dissonant counterpoint. This is not to say that the artistic and esthetic values of imitation have diminished but only that unrestrained accessibility increases the proclivity for unimaginative and mechanical usage. Contrapuntal manipulations not motivated by a genuine creative impulse quickly degenerate into a mere display of pedantry, but inspired contrapuntal writing remains today, as always, one of the composer's most versatile and esteemed modes of expression.

Though counterpoint and imitation are used almost synonymously, much effective contrapuntal music does not involve imitation. Contrapuntal associations of independent lines are difficult to classify and analyze, and it is for this reason that the following examples are drawn exclusively from imitative passages. They illustrate adaptations peculiar to the twentieth century of previously accepted practices, all of which persist to the present time. The one approach to counterpoint which is entirely a product of this century, the twelve-tone method, is the subject of the next chapter.

Direct Imitation

The first example, with its direct imitation at the octave after one beat, could have come from an earlier period except that it violates the principle, formerly observed, of resolving contrapuntal dissonances stepwise. Its twentieth-century origin is betrayed by the casual way the major seventh, augmented octave, and minor ninth are left by leap, but their dissonant effect is minimized by their being unaccented and of short duration.

Ex. 251 SHOSTAKOVICH: *Symphony No. 5* (1937) p3

Example 252 also has octave imitation at the distance of one beat and dissonances left by leap. Beginning the two parts together and making the upper one the follower by extending its first note is a novel touch.

Ex. 252 WALTON: *Belshazzar's Feast* (1931) p27

Imitative and nonimitative parts are often combined, as they are in Example 253. A descending line in thirds accompanies a curious bit of imitation replete with dissonances. The follower starts a half beat later in the measure than the leader, causing a shift in the metric stresses. All of the notes have the same letter name in the leader and follower, but seven of the eleven have different chromatic inflections.

Ex. 253 SCHOENBERG: *Pierrot Lunaire, No. 1—Mondestrunken* (1912)

The reasons which account for the preponderance of imitation at the fourth, fifth, and octave in earlier music no longer exist, so other intervals of imitation are used with equal freedom. In the exchange of thematic fragments between the two voices in Example 254 the imitation, allowing for enharmonic spellings, is at the minor ninth above and the major seventh below. In these transpositions the harmonic intervals are inverted, again allowing for enharmonic spellings, as they are in classic double (invertible) counterpoint at the octave.

Ex. 254 SCHOENBERG: *Verklaerte Nacht* (1899) p14

The fugal imitation shown in Example 255 is more recent but more conventional. The entrances at the fifth above and the octave below and the suspension-like resolutions of some of the dissonances could have come right out of Bach, but the lines and harmonies are less academic.

Ex. 255 HINDEMITH: *Ludus Tonalis—Fuga Octava in D* (1943)

Close fragmentary imitation producing pyramid effects is a common contemporary device illustrated in Example 256. The rising fifth in the first voice is imitated by fourths in the ensuing voices. In conventional music this would be tonal imitation, but in this case it is not used to preserve the tonality as it was during the common practice period. Successive entrances a major sixth, a major third, a major seventh, and an augmented fourth above the initial pitch lead to interesting vertical structures.

Ex. 256 KODALY: *Te Deum* (1936) p44

In the four-part imitation of Example 257 the first note of alternate entrances is transposed down an octave to avoid overlapping in the imitation, which otherwise is at the same pitch as the preceding voice. The third and fourth voices enter an octave lower than the first pair, and the distance between them is increased to two measures for added variety. The imitative counterpoint is followed with no break in the continuity by a thematic fragment in parallel seventh chords.

Ex. 257 BARTOK: *Piano Concerto No. 3* (1945) p59

Modified Imitation

The methods of thematic modification discussed in Chapter 12 are used imitatively, and Hindemith's *Ludus Tonalis* is virtually a catalog of these procedures. Example 258 begins with a fugue subject in its original form and in augmentation. Two measures later the augmented form enters in the soprano. In the seventh measure, while the augmented form is continuing in the soprano, the inverted form enters in the bass. The middle voice presents fragments from both the original and inverted forms of the subject.

Ex. 258 HINDEMITH: *Ludus Tonalis—Fuga Nona in B-flat* (1943)

The retrograde form of the fugue subject in Example 258 is partially
imitated by the retrograde inversion at the distance of one measure in
Example 259.

Ex. 259 HINDEMITH: *Ludus Tonalis—Fuga Nona in B-flat* (1943)

Slight deviations in imitating lines like those in the Hindemith examples just cited do not detract from the contrapuntal effect, but exact
imitation is usual when harmonic considerations are minimal as they are
in Example 260. Every interval in the second voice is a precise mirror
inversion of the corresponding interval in the first voice, though some are
spelled enharmonically.

Ex. 260 SCHOENBERG: *Pierrot Lunaire, No. 17—Parodie* (1912)

Less strict direct and mirror imitation are illustrated in Example 261. The third and fourth voices are in direct imitation at the octave. The second and fifth voices two octaves apart mirror the contour but not the intervals of the others. Bartok is one of the composers who is inclined to make compromises in imitation for the sake of sonority.

Ex. 261 BARTOK: *Piano Concerto No. 3* (1945) p32

The mirror imitation in Example 262 is subtly changed both rhythmically and melodically when the phrase is repeated with the top voice an octave higher. The imitating voice starts an eighth later than in the first phrase, but the fifth note is shortened an eighth to reestablish the original relationship between the parts. The 3/8 measure in the second phrase is a compressed version of the corresponding 2/4 measure. Concomitant with these rhythmic shifts, several notes in the second phrase imitation are a semitone higher than in the first phrase.

Ex. 262 BARTOK: *Mikrokosmos, No. 141—Subject and Reflection* (1926–37)

Simultaneous mirroring lacks the rhythmic interplay of imitation with a delayed entrance and of nonimitative counterpoint, but it is contrapuntally more interesting than melodic doubling to which it is related. The two parts in Example 263 create the impression of simultaneous mirroring, even though the intervals have been substantially adjusted to achieve the desired harmonic effect.

Ex. 263 BARTOK: *Concerto for Orchestra* (1943) p68

Example 264 is an intrinsically simple piece of writing which on closer examination reveals some intricate contrapuntal processes. In order of entrance, the second voice is an augmentation of the first; the third is an inversion of both, an augmentation of the first and a diminution of the second; and the fourth is an inversion of the third and a diminution of the second. In the second measure the procedure is repeated with the shapes of the motives reversed. The description of this passage sounds much more complicated than the music, which is convincing evidence of the contrapuntal mastery of the composer.

Ex. 264 BARTOK: *Piano Concerto No. 3* (1945) p36

The contrapuntal accomplishments of composers past and present can be fully appreciated only by those who have studied their works and attempted to duplicate their feats. The preceding examples and the following assignments show how some of the contrapuntal techniques have been and can be used in contemporary idioms. The sphere of composers is learning to use them; that of performers and listeners is learning to perceive and appreciate them.

Suggested Assignments

1. Locate and describe examples of imitation in twentieth-century compositions.
2. Using Example 251 as a model, write an exercise in two-part imitative counterpoint in which dissonances are treated freely.
   The following procedures facilitate writing imitative counterpoint:
   a. Start with an incisive motive and continue it for the distance of the imitation.
   b. Copy this line where it is to be in the imitation with the desired transposition and modifications, if any.
   c. Write a suitable counterpoint in the first voice which is also a logical continuation of the start.

d. Copy the new material in the second voice.

e. Repeat the process for the duration of the imitation.

3. Write a two-part exercise with imitation at a dissonant interval.

4. Write an exercise in which imitative lines are combined with a nonimitative line or an accompaniment.

5. Create a pyramid effect by a series of close imitative entrances using Example 256 as a model.

6. Add a simultaneous mirror to an original melody, adjusting the intervals as in Example 263 for the best harmonic effect.

7. Find or create a contemporary fugue subject and give its notation in the following forms: original, augmentation, diminution, inversion, retrograde, and retrograde inversion.

8. Write a brief example of two-part counterpoint with mirror imitation.

9. Write a brief example of two-part counterpoint with imitation in augmentation or diminution.

10. Compose a short work in two or three parts for the medium of your choice employing some of the contrapuntal procedures outlined in this chapter.

14

The Twelve-Tone Method

*T*HE *twelve-tone method* or *tone-row technique* is one of the most significant musical innovations of this century. Where the materials and procedures considered up to this point have been essentially extensions and modifications of previous practices, the serial techniques of the twelve-tone system constitute a basically new approach to composition. Its break with tradition was neither sudden nor absolute, but in this style of composition elements with no direct antecedents predominate. It was not, however, conceived as a revolt against tradition but rather as a means of unifying and systematizing tendencies already prevalent in music. These tendencies, previously observed, created certain problems for which the twelve-tone system was proposed as a solution. More than any other concept of comparable scope, its formulation as a method of composition was the work of a single mind, that of Arnold Schoenberg. Even if he had no other claim to fame, this achievement alone would assure his immortality in the realm of music.

The eventual impact of the twelve-tone method on the course of music history remains to be seen. Attitudes toward it have fluctuated radically during the past half century. At first it attracted only a handful of disciples within Schoenberg's immediate sphere of influence. Performances were rare, and the initial reaction of critics and audiences was negative if not openly hostile. The situation was not much improved until the end of World War II when the revitalized artistic atmosphere was auspicious for the ascendancy of the new style. Early serial works were rescued from obscurity, and Schoenberg, Berg, and Webern were hailed by some partisans as the greatest composers of their age and the only ones worthy of emulation. Legions of young composers adopted their methods and regarded any other approach to composition as passé. Some older composers (e. g., Stravinsky and Copland) turned to the twelve-tone method, and its pervasive influence can be detected in many works by nonserial composers. At its zenith serial control was extended to all elements of music. Though the pendulum now seems to be swinging back in the direction of less stringent controls, the twelve-tone system has left an indelible mark on twentieth-century musical thought. Consequently, knowledge of the methods and objectives of twelve-tone composition is valuable in the comprehension of contemporary music in general.

The aim of this chapter is to foster understanding of twelve-tone music and its rationale by developing a functional knowledge of the method. Those interested in pursuing the study further will find several books listed under Suggested Assignment 1 at the end of the chapter which deal with the subject exclusively or exhaustively.

To understand the twelve-tone method one must first understand the situation which engendered it. Early in the century musical materials were expanded to the point where the foundations of conventional tonal organization (tonality, scales, and root progressions) were being shaken. Several of the contributing factors have been examined in previous chapters. Some composers were content to extend the resources within recognizable limits which preserved essential structural functions. The concept of tonality could be broadened without being lost. Extensive chromaticism and the substitution of modal and synthetic scales for major and minor would not necessarily dissipate the values of selective scales. Increasingly complex sonorities could be introduced, and chord roots could move freely without becoming unintelligible. Within these boundaries traditional methods of tonal organization were adequate. Other composers were inclined to traverse these boundaries in the pursuit of tonal relationships without tonality, not based on selective scales, using tonal aggregates indescribable in conventional terms, and dissonance almost to the exclusion of consonance. Under these circumstances conventional methods of tonal organization ceased to function. To replace them Schoenberg devised "A Method of Composing with Twelve Tones which Are Related only with One Another." This is the method commonly referred to as the twelve-tone, note series, or tone-row technique, system, or method.

Formation of the Series

In strict twelve-tone music all pitch relationships are governed by a predetermined note series consisting of the twelve tones of a tempered chromatic scale in a fixed linear order without repetitions. The crux of the series lies in the disposition of the twelve tones and the resulting intervals between them. The original German term for the twelve tones in their established order, *Reihe,* is variously translated as *series, row,* or *set.* In the abstract, the series is usually represented in notes of equal value within a limited compass. The first version is designated as the *original form, basic set,* or *prime* to distinguish it from other versions and transpositions.

There are no definite rules regarding the formation of the series, but a few principles beyond the requirement of using all twelve tones with no repetitions are generally observed. Groups of notes with tonal implications are ordinarily avoided to preserve the atonal nature of the style. Except when the number or type of intervals is limited for a special purpose, a variety of interval relationships between the notes of the series is usual. The series of Examples 265 and 266 are typical in this respect with five different intervals in each. These intervals and their inversions, available through octave transposition of one of the notes, comprise eight of the eleven possible. In Example 265 the tritone, the minor third, and its inversion are missing. In Example 266 the tritone, the major second, and its inversion are missing.

Ex. 265 SCHOENBERG: *String Quartet No. 4* (1936)

Ex. 266 KRENEK: *Twelve Short Piano Pieces* (1938)

The possibilities for series formations are almost infinite. For maximum variety all eleven intervals can be incorporated in the series, though half will be inversions of the other half. More often, for added unity, characteristic interval relationships are repeated, as in Example 265. In this series, notes 8–9–10 are a retrograde inversion of notes 1–2–3 transposed, and notes 10–11–12 are a transposed mirror of notes 3–4–5. This series is also constructed so that under certain operations the opposite halves of two forms of the series will contain different permutations of the same six notes.

The series of Example 267, shown as it appears in the solo violin part, contains a limited number of characteristic intervals. It has only thirds and major seconds, one spelled enharmonically as a diminished third. Enharmonic spellings are used indiscriminately in twelve-tone music. Any three consecutive notes in the first nine form a triad, and all four triad types—major, minor, augmented and diminished—are represented.

Ex. 267 BERG: *Violin Concerto* (1935) p4

Variants of the Series

A basic premise of twelve-tone theory is that the series retains its identity and continues to function in all of its linear forms: *original* (O), *inversion* (I), *retrograde* (R), and *retrograde inversion* (RI). The four linear forms of the series introduced in Example 265 are shown in Example 268. Observe that the inversion is specifically a mirror inversion of the original, not the type of inversion produced by octave transposition of one of the notes in an interval. The original form of the series at its initial pitch level is designated by the symbol O–1. The symbol I–1 designates the inversion starting on the same note or its octave, and the symbols R–1 and RI–1 designate the untransposed retrograde forms of the original and the inversion respectively.

Ex. 268 SCHOENBERG: *String Quartet No. 4* (1936)

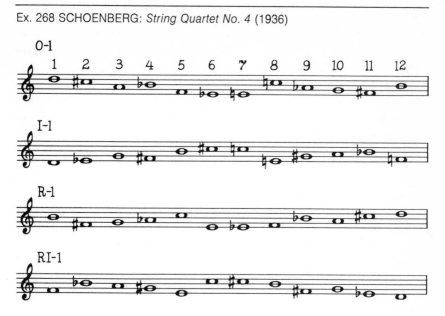

Each of the four forms of the series is available at all twelve pitch levels. Transpositions are indicated by numbers showing the relationship to the initial pitch levels as follows:[1]

> 1 = initial pitch level
> 2 = up a minor second, down a major seventh
> 3 = up a major second, down a minor seventh
> 4 = up a minor third, down a major sixth
> 5 = up a major third, down a minor sixth
> 6 = up a perfect fourth, down a perfect fifth
> 7 = up or down a tritone
> 8 = up a perfect fifth, down a perfect fourth
> 9 = up a minor sixth, down a major third
> 10 = up a major sixth, down a minor third
> 11 = up a minor seventh, down a major second
> 12 = up a major seventh, down a minor second

The twelve transpositions of the four forms of the series bring the total number of possible variants to forty-eight, though it is unusual

---

1. In some publications the notes of the series and the transpositions are numbered 0-11 rather than 1-12, and the original form of the series is designated the *prime* (P).

for all of them to be used in a composition. *Set-complex* is the designation for the forty-eight variants of the series collectively. The complete set-complex of any series can be represented efficiently by arranging the letter names of the notes for the various forms and transpositions in a 12×12 checkerboard pattern according to the following procedure. Write the notes of the original series at the initial pitch level in the squares of the top line. Next write the notes of the inversion down the first column starting from the note already in the first square. Complete the chart by writing in each line the transposition of the original which starts with the note of the inversion in the first column. The completed chart will then give all transpositions of the original reading from left to right, of the retrograde reading from right to left, of the inversion reading from top to bottom, and of the retrograde inversion reading from bottom to top. Having a chart like this showing all variants of the series at a glance is an invaluable tool when composing or analyzing twelve-tone music. A chart of the Schoenberg *Fourth String Quartet* set-complex is given as a model. In this and all similarly constructed set-complex charts the note in the top left corner appears in a diagonal line to the opposite corner, and the pitches of the corner notes on the other axis are equidistant above and below their counterparts.

Ex. 269 SCHOENBERG: *String Quartet No. 4* (1936)

O ——▶   ◀—— R

I											I
D	C♯	A	B♭	F	E♭	E	C	A♭	G	F♯	B
E♭	D	B♭	B	F♯	E	F	C♯	A	A♭	G	C
G	F♯	D	E♭	B♭	A♭	A	F	C♯	C	B	E
F♯	F	C♯	D	A	G	G♯	E	C	B	B♭	E♭
B	B♭	F♯	G	D	C	C♯	A	F	E	E♭	A♭
C♯	C	G♯	A	E	D	D♯	B	G	F♯	F	B♭
C	B	G	A♭	E♭	D♭	D	B♭	G♭	F	E	A
E	D♯	B	C	G	F	F♯	D	B♭	A	G♯	C♯
G♯	G	E♭	E	B	A	B♭	F♯	D	C♯	C	F
A	G♯	E	F	C	B♭	B	G	E♭	D	C♯	F♯
B♭	A	F	F♯	C♯	B	C	G♯	E	E♭	D	G
F	E	C	C♯	G♯	F♯	G	E♭	B	B♭	A	D

RI   RI

O ——▶   ◀—— R

Twelve-Tone Themes

The determination of the series and its variants is a precompositional procedure in twelve-tone music. The set-complex is the source of all pitch relationships, thematic as well as nonthematic, but the series itself is not a theme in any ordinary sense. Before becoming a theme it must have a distinctive rhythm and contour. In deriving a theme from the series, certain liberties are customary. Notes may be used in any octave and may be repeated freely as long as the order is not disturbed. A theme can be constructed from segments of the series, with the remaining notes assigned to subsidiary parts, or its notes can be drawn from more than one variant. Theme and phrase divisions may or may not coincide with statements of the series. Examples 270–275 illustrate with exceptional clarity the derivation of multiple twelve-tone themes from the same basic series.

Ex. 270 SCHOENBERG: *String Quartet No. 4* (1936) p1

The tritone transposition of the original series, O–7, is the basis for Example 271. The rhythm is identical with that of Example 270, but the contour is altered by placing some of the notes in different octaves.

Ex. 271 SCHOENBERG: *String Quartet No. 4* (1936) p18

Example 272 derived from the O–11 form of the series has a new rhythm and an entirely different character. In addition to repeated notes it has another permissible type of repetition, that of a small fragment. G-flat and F, notes 9 and 10 in this transposition of the series, are repeated before notes 11 and 12 appear. Repetitions of this sort involving small groups of notes perceived as a unit are admitted freely in lines and accompaniment patterns, as are trills, tremolos, and embellishing figures.

Ex. 272 SCHOENBERG: *String Quartet No. 4* (1936) p63

In Example 273 the I–4 form of the series is united with the rhythm associated with the O–1 and O–7 forms in Examples 270 and 271. The reiteration of a scheme of time values can be equated with the reiteration of pitch patterns predicated upon a series. Though different contours and row forms are sometimes combined with the same rhythm in the works of Schoenberg, the systematic serialization of durations is an innovation attributed to the second generation of twelve-tone composers (e. g., Boulez and Stockhausen).

Ex. 273 SCHOENBERG: *String Quartet No. 4* (1936) p10

The pitches in Example 274 are from the R–1 form of the series. The rhythm has features in common with the preceding example, but the entire pattern is not duplicated.

Ex. 274 SCHOENBERG: *String Quartet No. 4* (1936) p1

Example 275 is a rhythmically independent theme derived from the RI–1 form of the series.

Ex. 275 SCHOENBERG: *String Quartet No. 4* (1936) p30

The procedures observed in the construction of twelve-tone themes are equally valid for any and all serial lines, subsidiary as well as principal.

Twelve-Tone Texture

The foregoing examples demonstrate the application of the twelve-tone method to the formation of single lines. In strict twelve-tone composition not just the thematic material but the entire texture is derived from the same series. Twelve-tone composition is primarily a contrapuntal procedure, so attention is focused on the construction and combination of lines. Freedom in the treatment of its vertical aspects compensates for the strict adherence to the order of the series in all parts. Sonority, as a phenomenon independent of linear combinations, is of so little importance in the style that principles of harmonic structure and harmonic progression are not given by its theorists, nor are harmonic formulas detectable in the compositions.

Notes which sound together, termed *simultaneities* in some twelve-tone references, may consist of any vertical arrangement of any number of notes from the series. A simultaneity results when notes in multiple lines coincide rhythmically or when a segment of the series is sounded as a chord. Contrapuntal lines can be derived from the same form or different forms of the series. In verticalized segments the linear ordering may be preserved from top to bottom or bottom to top, but this is not a requirement. Spacing is adjusted to secure the desired sonorous effect. Octaves and unisons are generally avoided, as are clusters and congestions. Conventional consonant chords occur but rarely and are permitted only when they have little connotation of tonality. All simultaneities are rationalized in terms of the series, but the series can be manipulated to produce virtually any combination of tones. Some series are constructed with a view to the harmonic value of certain groups of consecutive notes.

Though sonority is a secondary consideration, it is not ignored by twelve-tone composers. Climactic points in the form and in the lines are associated with increased tension and density in the vertical structure.

198

Harmonic tension is related to dissonance, but the two cannot be considered synonymous. Other factors such as spacing, scoring, dynamics, rhythm, and tempo also influence tension.

The degree of dissonance can be reckoned roughly by the number and kind of dissonant intervals comprised between all component parts. Seconds and sevenths are dissonant. Minor seconds and major sevenths are more dissonant than major seconds and minor sevenths. Perfect fourths are consonant or dissonant depending upon the context. In combination with other intervals their effect usually is that of a consonance. Tritones are dissonant, but in atonal music they do not demand the prescribed resolution associated with them in tonal music. The other intervals are consonant.

Chords and linear textures can be derived from the series in several ways. The notes of one form of the series can be distributed between all of the parts. The melody can be based on one segment and the accompaniment on another segment of the same form. It is also possible for different forms of the series to be in progress concurrently. Each part can have its own form, or the pitches of the different forms can be distributed between the various parts since completing a series in the same part is not required.

The foregoing generalizations are oversimplified but sufficiently valid to serve as a guide for initiates analyzing or composing twelve-tone music. Specific applications of the method in a mature work by its originator are illustrated in the following analyses of excerpts from Schoenberg's *Violin Concerto*. Example 276 gives the forms of the series used in Examples 277–279. The first line is the basic set at its original pitch level (O–1). The next three lines are the inversion (I–6), the retrograde (R–1), and the retrograde inversion (RI–6) at the pitch of their initial appearance in the concerto. The last two lines are the original form (O–8) and the inverted form (I–1) in the transpositions used at the beginning of the second movement. The last movement begins with the same forms and transpositions of the series as the first movement, paralleling the key relationship of tonal music. The series forms are used in pairs—O–1 with I–6, R–1 with RI–6, and O–8 with I–1. The interval between the first notes of the O and I pairs and between the last notes of the R and RI pair is a perfect fourth. Between corresponding halves of these pairs no pitch is duplicated. Consequently, the pitch content (but not the order) of opposite halves is identical. A series with special relationships of this type between segments is called a *combinatorial set* by Milton Babbitt, in whose writings the theory of combinatoriality is explored in depth.

Ex. 276 SCHOENBERG: *Violin Concerto* (1936)

The complete series in its original form is distributed between the solo part and the accompaniment in the upbeat and the first three measures of Example 277. The minor seconds between notes 1–2 and 7–8 of the series are treated sequentially. The harmonic intervals formed by notes 9–10 and 11–12 are repeated alternately at the end of the first phrase and again at the end of the second phrase.

The I–6 form of the series is the basis of measures 4–7. The solo part again has notes 1–2 and 7–8 of the series, and their rhythmic treatment produces a free mirror of the line in the first phrase.

In measures 8–11 the full series in its original form appears in the solo part. This appearance establishes the order of the notes in the series, since it is not possible to determine in the prior statements which of the notes sounded together comes first. The original form in the violin is accompanied by the nonduplicating segments of the inversion (I–6).

The solo and the accompaniment exchange forms of the series in measure 11. The violin plays the first six notes of the inversion in the rhythm associated with the original form in the preceding phrase, and then completes the series in a nonrepetitive rhythm. This statement of the inverted form is accompanied by the material of measures 1–4 rhythmically compressed and with some additional repetitions of harmonic intervals.

200

The bass is the opening solo line transposed down an octave and with the long durations shortened.

The retrograde form of the series first appears starting in measure 15. Distributed between the parts, it is completed in measure 16. The retrograde inversion (RI–6) follows immediately, also distributed between the parts.

The original form reappears in measure 20. In this statement the first six notes in the melody are accompanied by two three-note chords using the remaining six notes. The same procedure is repeated starting in measure 21 using the I–6 form of the series.

Ex. 277 SCHOENBERG: *Violin Concerto* (1936) p3 (beginning)

Ex. 277 (continued)

Example 278, from the beginning of the second movement, is based on the O–8 and I–1 forms of the series. These transpositions, down a fourth or up a fifth from those at the beginning of the first movement, correspond with the key change for second movements in tonal music. The series is now treated somewhat more freely, perhaps on the assumption that by this time it is familiar. One statement of the original form occupies the solo violin for twelve measures. The first six notes are accompanied by the nonduplicating segment (notes 1–6) of the inversion repeated four times. The remaining six notes of the original are similarly accompanied by repetitions of the other six-note segment of the inversion, which is likewise nonduplicating.

The *finale* begins as shown in Example 279 with the same forms of the series as the first movement and with procedures reminiscent of those in the second movement. In this case five repetitions of the first half and four repetitions of the second half of O–1 accompany a single extended statement of I–6 in the solo part. The four-note chords in the accompaniment are good examples of verticalized segments of the series.

Anton Webern, who was a student of Schoenberg, applied the principles of serial composition in a very personal way. His style matured slowly over a period of years. It is characterized by extremely sparse texture and highly concentrated motivic structure. His works, which invariably are of short duration, create the impression of having been distilled to the point where only the barest essentials remain. He found the intimate mediums of musical expression most congenial and wrote extensively for voice accompanied by piano or a small group of instruments and for uniquely constituted chamber ensembles.

Ex. 278 SCHOENBERG: *Violin Concerto* (1936) p29

Ex. 279 SCHOENBERG: *Violin Concerto* (1936) p45

Example 280 is representative of Webern's mature style. The score showing the full instrumentation of his *Symphony* is necessary to convey an impression of the writing and scoring, which are inseparable in Webern. The discontinuity with more rests than notes, the angularity of the lines with wide leaps spanning dissonant intervals, the pointillistic scattering of notes over the page, and the subdued dynamics are all typical. Full tuttis and fortissimos are hardly to be found in his scores. The

Ex. 280 WEBERN: *Symphony* (1928) p1

contrapuntal procedures and strict adherence to the twelve-tone method are also Webern characteristics. The excerpt shows the beginning of a double canon with both followers in contrary motion. The first canon leader starts on A in the second horn and after four notes continues in the clarinet. The inverted follower begins two measures later on the same pitch in the first horn. The second canon leader starts on F (a major third below A) in the harp, moves immediately to the cello for three notes, then to the second violin for one, and back to the harp. Its inverted follower also begins in the harp but on C-sharp (a major third above A), and then the three cello notes are imitated in the viola. Similar procedures continue for the remainder of the movement up to the coda, which is a two-part canon.

Experience with other kinds of music does not provide the background needed to evaluate twelve-tone music properly. Because of its special nature, familiarity with the method and with representative works is necessary before listeners are equipped to evaluate it, performers to interpret it, and composers to decide whether to adopt, modify, or reject its premises. No matter what one's attitude toward serialism is, he will have illustrious company. It has been praised as the only valid contemporary idiom and condemned as a sterile, mechanistic surrogate for creativity. The eventual status of the twelve-tone system in the history of music is yet to be determined, but its influence on the music of the past fifty years has been enormous. In the future, students may study the method and write atonal exercises as routinely as they now study tonal harmony and counterpoint and write exercises in major and minor keys. Such curricular changes conceivably could bring to dodecaphonic works the understanding and perhaps the acceptance by listening audiences that thus far have eluded them, but present indications are that they will remain consigned to the esoteric niche they now occupy by the very qualities that distinguish them.

Suggested Assignments

1. The following is a selected list of sources for supplementary reading assignments:

   Brindle, Reginald Smith. *Serial Composition.* London: Oxford University Press, 1966.

   Krenek, Ernst. *Studies in Counterpoint.* New York: G. Schirmer, 1940.

   Leibowitz, René. *Schoenberg and His School.* Translated by Dika Newlin. 1949. Reprint. New York: Da Capo Press, 1970.

Perle, George. *Serial Composition and Atonality*. 3d. ed., rev. Berkeley: University of California Press, 1972.

Rufer, Josef. *Composition with Twelve Notes Related Only to One Another*. Translated by Humphrey Searle. 1954. Reprint. New York: Dover Publications.

Searle, Humphrey. *Twentieth Century Counterpoint*. London: Williams and Norgate, 1954.

2. Listen to the recorded lecture-demonstration *Twelve-Tone Composition,* Folkways FT3612.
3. Make a checkerboard table like Example 269 for the Schoenberg *Violin Concerto* series (see Example 276) or for the series of a twelve-tone work you are preparing to analyze.
4. Analyze in the manner of Examples 277–280 passages from selected twelve-tone compositions.
5. Write several series using Example 265, 266, 268, and 276 as models.
6. Prepare a checkerboard table like Example 269 for one of the series you have written, and then compose several themes based on the series using Examples 270–275 as models. Repeat the series or combine different forms to make longer themes.
7. Using only the 0–1 form of the series, write a two-part exercise with the notes of the series distributed between the parts.
8. Using any two forms of the series, write a two-part exercise.
9. Write a twelve-tone exercise which has simultaneities (chords) of three or more notes.
10. Write a short twelve-tone composition employing the method in any way you deem to be appropriate. Make an analysis as you compose.

15

Total Organization

THE post-Webern serialists aiming toward the *total organization* of musical materials have extended the concepts of the "classical" twelve-tone system beyond pitch to bring other elements of music under serial control. These other elements—now called *parameters*, borrowing a term from mathematics—include rhythm (durations), tempo (speed levels), dynamics (degrees of loudness), articulation (modes of attack), density (number of parts), and spacing (octave distribution). As a rule the initial pitch series is transformed by some rational method into an order of values applicable to the other serially controlled parameters. The procedures vary from composer to composer and from work to work, but the possibilities which have been used include deriving the values of the other series from the notes, intervals, and frequencies of the pitch series. Another procedure is to establish an independent, arbitrary order for each serially controlled aspect of the music. To avoid the excessive uniformity of configuration that might otherwise result from the strict ordering of several parameters concurrently, the order within a given series is sometimes subjected to systematic and progressive rotation. The rotation plan and the choice and arrangement of components can be serially governed to produce music in which the sound events are essentially predetermined by a system conceived and set in motion by the composer. The compositional process begins with the composer's determination of the various elements, series, and operations to be employed. The next step is to execute the predetermined serial operations. The third and final stage is to make decisions regarding those dimensions of the music not automatically predetermined and to make adjustments, to the extent they are allowed, in those that are. Ernst Krenek is an active composer and lucid apologist for this new serialism. His article "Extents and Limits of Serial Techniques" in the *Musical Quarterly* 46/2 (1960)[1] describes the serial procedures in several representative works in the genre.

The methods of serializing elements other than pitch are not standardized. On the contrary, composers who employ multiple serial controls in their efforts to organize sound events by completely rational means display a definite proclivity for unique approaches. In this respect Milton Babbitt is no exception. The procedures regulating the pitches, dynamics, and durations in his *Three Compositions for Piano* are peculiar to that work, but they provide an excellent introduction to the concept of total organization.

In Babbitt's *Three Compositions for Piano, No. 1*[2] the pitches are derived from four pairs of combinatorially related forms of the series in which the pitch content of corresponding hexachords is mutually exclusive. All eight forms of the series are exposed in measures 1–8, with nonduplicating segments of a different pair in each measure as shown in Example 281. Each transformation of the series is consistently associated with a dynamic level—original with *mp*, retrograde with *mf*, inversion with *f*, and retrograde inversion with *p*—until the final entry, where each dynamic level is lowered two degrees. The transformation of the pitch series, therefore, dictates the dynamic level at each moment, and changes in intensity delineate statements of the pitch series.

In formulating the duration series a sixteenth value is taken as the basic unit. An arbitrary grouping of the units, 5 1 4 2, becomes the original form of the series. The total number of units in the series is twelve, corresponding with the twelve pitches, and the total of each half is six, corresponding with the hexachords. Reversing the order of the original series produces the retrograde, 2 4 1 5. The relationship between the groups in the original duration series and their inversion is much like the relationship between intervals and their inversions. Where the total number of semitones in an interval and its inversion equals twelve, the total number of units in a rhythmic group and its inversion is determined to be six. Subtracting each value of the original series from six produces the inversion, 1 5 2 4. Reversing the order of the inversion produces the retrograde inversion, 4 2 5 1. The properties of the original are preserved in the permutations. Each rhythmic group is expressed by a corresponding number of sixteenth notes or their equivalent, except that

1. Reprinted in *Problems of Modern Music*, Paul Henry Lang, ed. (W. W. Norton, 1962).

2. Included in Charles Burkhart's *Anthology for Musical Analysis*, 2d ed. (Holt, Rinehart and Winston, 1972). For a more complete analysis see George Perle's *Serial Composition and Atonality*, 3d ed., rev. (University of California Press, 1972).

the last note of a group may be prolonged. Terminal prolongations, rests, accents, and phrasing marks serve to articulate the groups, but they are not always defined. Transformations of the duration series are invariably associated with the corresponding transformation of the pitch series, and in turn with a dynamic level as follows:

Pitch Series	Duration Series	Dynamic Level
$\left. \begin{array}{l} 0-1 \\ 0-7 \end{array} \right\}$		*mp*
$\left. \begin{array}{l} R-1 \\ R-7 \end{array} \right\}$		*mf*
$\left. \begin{array}{l} I-2 \\ I-8 \end{array} \right\}$		*f*
$\left. \begin{array}{l} RI-2 \\ RI-8 \end{array} \right\}$		*p*

The forms of the pitch series are identified and the duration groups bracketed in the following excerpt from the work. Accidentals affect only those notes which they immediately precede, except when notes are tied.

Ex. 281 BABBITT: *Three Compositions for Piano, No. 1* (1948)

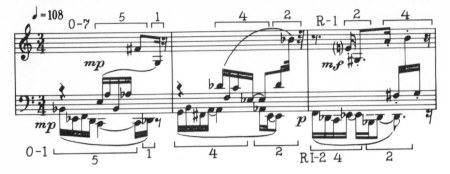

The serial controls in *Structure Ia* by Pierre Boulez are more extensive and complex than those employed by Babbitt. A thorough analysis by Gyorgy Ligeti in *Die Reihe, No. 4* (Theodore Presser, 1960) was used as a reference in preparing the following summary of its salient features. The pitch series is borrowed from Messiaen's 1949 piano composition *Modes de valeurs et d'intensités*. The notes of the original series are numbered consecutively, and these numbers represent the same notes in all permuta-

212

tions of the pitch series. The original duration series is produced by multiplying a thirty-second value by factors from 1 to 12 in order. There are
twelve progressive degrees of intensity from *pppp* to *ffff* , though only
ten are used, and ten modes of attack corresponding with the ten degrees
of intensity actually used. The original forms of the four series are shown
in Example 282. The numbers function in the same way with the other
parameters as they do with pitch. That is, each number represents a
specific note, duration, intensity, and mode of attack, not a position in
the series. This system of numbering enables Boulez to represent all
serially controlled parameters numerically and to use the same numerical
tables for different parameters.

Ex. 282 BOULEZ: *Structures, Ia* (1955)

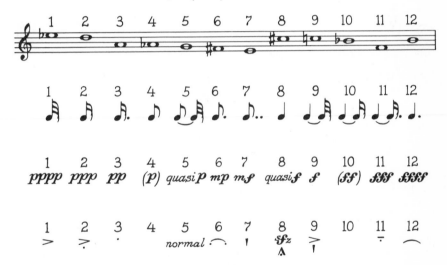

Boulez arranged the forty-eight forms of the pitch series represented
numerically in two checkerboard patterns, one for the twenty-four original and retrograde transpositions and the other for the twenty-four
inversion and retrograde inversion transpositions. The resulting numerical tables are the source of forty-eight equivalent forms of the duration
series. The succession of intensities and modes of attack are predicated
upon the sequence of numbers in certain diagonal lines in the numerical
tables. Each form of the pitch series is combined with a different permutation of the duration series in a unique serial thread which is used once and

Ex. 283 BOULEZ: *Structures: Ia* (1955) p1

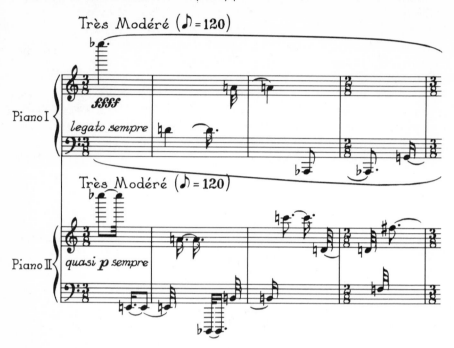

only once. The intensity and mode of attack are constant for each thread. The forty-eight threads are distributed in fourteen sections with from one to six threads beginning and ending simultaneously in each section. Example 283 shows the first section consisting of two threads. The thread in Piano I combines the O–1 pitch series with an RI permutation of the duration series:

$$12 \quad 11 \quad 9 \quad 10 \quad 3 \quad 6 \quad 7 \quad 1 \quad 2 \quad 8 \quad 4 \quad 5$$

The intensity, *ffff*, and the slurred mode of attack are both 12 in their respective series. The thread in Piano II combines the I–1 pitch series with an R permutation of the duration series:

$$5 \quad 8 \quad 6 \quad 4 \quad 3 \quad 9 \quad 2 \quad 1 \quad 7 \quad 11 \quad 10 \quad 12$$

The intensity, *quasi p*, and the "normal" mode of attack are both 5 in their respective series.

In *Structure Ia* a rational plan of organization also extends to the ordering of serial forms, determining the overall structure, and to such parameters as density, register distribution, and tempos. The sound events are substantially governed by predetermined serial procedures, an approach to composition implied by the designation *total organization*. With the advent of total organization the twelve-tone system seems to have reached its culmination, pending possible future serial developments in the areas of electronic and computer music.

Suggested Assignments

1. Read an article or a section in a book dealing with some aspect of total organization or a totally organized work.
2. Complete the analysis of Babbitt's *Three Compositions for Piano, No. 1* using Example 281 as a model.
3. Devise a method for deriving a duration series from a pitch series and write out a representative number of integrated permutations of the series in which the pitches and durations are combined.
4. Compose a piece using the pitch and duration series of Assignment 3 in which these two parameters, at least, are serially controlled and related.

16

Microtones

$\mathcal{M}$ ICROTONES (intervals smaller than a semitone) occur in the music of several primitive and oriental cultures, and they have interested composers and theorists of the Western world since the time of the ancient Greeks. Those of our century are no exception, and some of them regard microtones as the next logical step in the evolution of our musical system. Composers and theorists of this persuasion are motivated by different reasons and propose diverse solutions to the problems of microtonal music.

Microtonal embellishments have been used incidentally in works which otherwise are confined to conventional pitches. Bartok's *Violin Concerto* and *Sixth String Quartet* are two of these. He indicates quarter-tone inflections above and below standard pitches by arrows pointing in the direction of the deviation. In Example 284 the C-sharps with the arrows pointing up are midway between a normal C-sharp and D in pitch. The E-flats with the arrows pointing down are midway between a normal E-flat and D in pitch. In other words, the arrows raise or lower the pitch a quarter tone. Arrows apply within measures like sharps and flats and are canceled by a bar line, a natural, or a sharp or a flat sign without an arrow.

Ex. 284 BARTOK: *Violin Concerto* (1938) p45

Ernest Bloch uses microtones similarly in his *Quintet for Piano and Strings,* but the notation is different. Diagonal lines positioned before the notes like sharps and flats are used instead of arrows. A line slanting up raises the pitch a quarter tone, and a line slanting down lowers the pitch a quarter tone. A diagonal line appears before each note thus inflected, not just the first of each measure, so no sign is required to cancel the quarter-tone symbols. Only raised quarter tones occur in Example 285, but lowered quarter tones appear elsewhere in the work.

Ex. 285 BLOCH: *Quintet* (1923) p2

The makeshift notation used for sporadic microtones is inadequate for music which is consistently microtonal. The five-line staff designed for seven notes and already taxed by twelve is not readily adaptable to the notation of microtones. However, adaptations of conventional notation have been used for quarter-tone music by several composers. The additional pitches are indicated by supplementary symbols placed before notes like sharps and flats. Quarter-tone signs vary in detail from composer to composer and sometimes even from work to work. Most are modified forms of the basic sharp and flat signs. Modifications include adding appendages to the standard symbols, leaving open and reversing the body of flat signs, and varying the number of strokes in sharp signs.

The quarter-tone notation of Alois Haba shown in Example 286 is typical. His *Fantasy for Violin Solo in Quarter Tones* is recorded on Folkways FM3355.

Ex. 286 HABA: *Quarter-Tone Scale Notation*

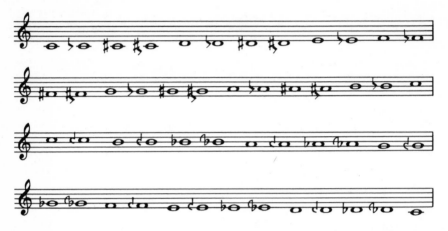

Penderecki uses quarter-tone symbols with different shapes but the same functions in his *Passion and Death of Our Lord Jesus Christ According to St. Luke.*

†	quarter-tone sharp
‡	three-quarter-tone sharp
♭	quarter-tone flat
ↄ	three-quarter-tone flat

All but the quarter-tone flat appear in the following solo soprano line. The X-shaped note heads indicate *"quasi recitando."*

Ex. 287 PENDERECKI: *Passion According to St. Luke* (1965) p18

The inability of composers writing quarter-tone music to agree on a common system of notation limits the accessibility of their music. Performers are understandably reluctant to master a complicated system of notation peculiar to a single work or composer. The adoption of standardized notation is perequisite to more significant achievements in quarter-tone music. Whether the system should be that of Haba and the others who continue to use the five-line staff or a new system designed specifically for quarter tones is as yet undecided.

Also undecided is the optimum size for microtones. Scales of 24 quarter tones are only one possibility. Ferruccio Busoni advocated a 36-tone scale with sixths of a tone as the smallest interval. Haba developed a system for notating intervals as small as twelfths of a tone, 72 to an octave, but at latest word he had not utilized intervals this small in compositions. Haba notated his 72-tone scale on a conventional staff with signs used in the manner of sharps and flats, but a totally new approach would seem to be more promising for notating microtones this small.

Julian Carrillo devised one such system which combines precision and flexibility. The note C is represented by the figure 0 (zero). Equal intervals above C are numbered consecutively up to the total within an octave. A chromatic (twelve-tone) scale would be notated with the numbers 0 through 11. A quarter-tone (24-tone) scale would use the numbers 0 through 23. Busoni's 36-tone scale would require the numbers 0 through 35, and the 96-tone scale used by Carrillo in his *Preludio a*

Cristobal Colón employs the numbers 0 through 95. Numbers representing pitches in the octave above middle C are placed on a single line. Numbers above and below the line denote pitches in the next higher and lower octaves, respectively. Still higher and lower octaves are shown by numbers on, above, and below lines that appear and function like ledger lines.

Example 288 shows the pitches of a two-octave G major scale notated in two ways using Carrillo's system. The scale is written using numbers appropriate for conventional semitones, twelve to an octave. Then the same pitches are represented by the numbers used for Carrillo's 96-tone scale. Consecutive numbers in this notation would indicate intervals equal to one-sixteenth of a tone.

Ex. 288 CARRILLO: *G Major Scale Notation*

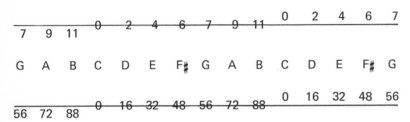

In Carrillo's notation stems, flags, and beams are attached to the numbers for the shorter rhythmic values. A bent stem indicates a half note and no stem a whole note. Dotted numbers are like dotted notes in conventional notation. A slanted wavy line between numbers indicates a glissando, and a vertical wavy line indicates an arpeggiated chord. Example 289 shows the appearance of a Carrillo score. Unfortunately the recording of this revolutionary work is out of print, but his microtonal *Mass for Pope John XXIII* (1962) can be heard on Composers Recording S-246.

Ex. 289 CARRILLO: *Preludio a Cristobal Colón* (1934) p7

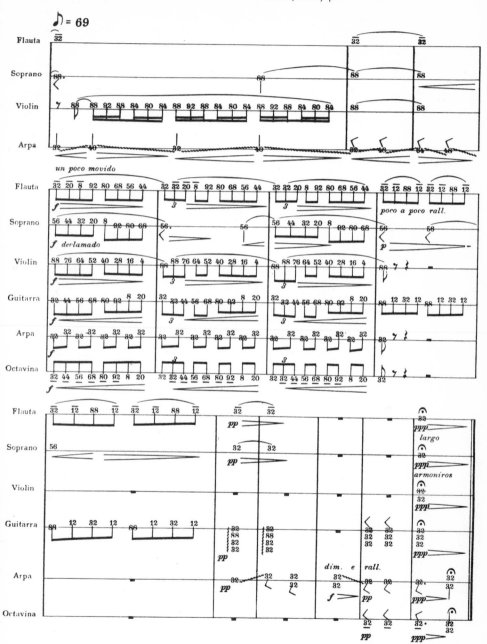

The microtones mentioned thus far have been derived from octaves or tempered whole tones fractionally divided into equal intervals. Joseph Yasser describes a different way of arriving at a scale with more than twelve tones to an octave. In his book *A Theory of Evolving Tonality* (American Library of Musicology, 1932, out of print), he rejects the arbitrary and mechanical splitting of equal intervals into smaller units and advocates extending scale resources by the evolutionary processes he perceives in the music of the past. He traces the evolution of scales from the pentatonic scale to the seven-tone scale and from the seven-tone scale to the twelve-tone scale. The next step in this evolutionary process, according to Yasser, is a nineteen-tone scale. Of the nineteen tones, the twelve now in general use would be "regular" scale degrees corresponding to the seven diatonic notes, and the seven new tones would be "auxiliary" scale degrees corresponding to the five chromatic notes.

Meantone fifths, slightly smaller than acoustically perfect fifths, provide the basis for a 31-tone scale. Thirty-one meantone fifths superimposed form a virtual cycle, and by minute expansion form a perfect cycle just as twelve tempered fifths do. That is, the thirty-second tone in the one series and the thirteenth in the other duplicate the starting note eighteen and seven octaves higher, respectively. Meantone fifths were the basis of an early tuning system, yielding acoustically perfect major thirds, so there is historical precedent for this modification of the fifth. Proponents of this system point not only to the expanded resources of the 31-tone scale but to the improved tuning of conventional intervals as well.

In Harry Partch's book *Genesis of a Music* (second edition, Da Capo Press, 1973) tuning systems and scale constructions are examined in detail and evidence is presented supporting the superiority of a 43-tone scale of unequal intervals based on ratios. Partch has designed and constructed numerous instruments, developed a unique notational system appropriate for the tonal materials and the individual instruments, trained performers, and produced a quantity of music utilizing the resources of this 43-tone scale. To experience the full impact of Partch's creations they must be seen as well as heard, but the aural aspects of his music are effectively captured on the recording of his *Delusion of the Fury* (Columbia M2–30576). A demonstration record of the instruments with commentary by Partch and a booklet with color photographs included with the album provide a more effective introduction to Partch's artistic achievements than is possible without sound and color.

Partch, who has achieved widespread recognition only recently, has devoted a lifetime to solving the theoretical, aesthetic, technical, and practical problems of 43-tone music (he shuns the term "microtonal").

This fact dramatizes the magnitude of the problems, which are similar for any music based on intervals smaller than a semitone. Not only is a new system of notation required, but new instruments and uniquely trained performers as well. While voices, string instruments, and trombones are capable of producing microtones, tuning precision is contingent upon the accuracy of human responses. Teachers accustomed to reminding students to sing or play semitonal music "in tune" are sure to be horrified by the prospect of teaching them to perform microtonal music. Radical modifications are necessary to expand the pitch capabilities of instruments with keys, valves, or frets. These problems exist, naturally, only for the microtonal music involving live performers and conventional means of sound production with which we are concerned at the moment. The electronic mediums considered in Chapter 19 are intrinsically microtonal, and with them performance and notational problems are bypassed.

Excluding electronic instruments, two pianos tuned a quarter tone apart or a single instrument with two keyboards and two sets of strings tuned a quarter tone apart probably provide the most practical performance mediums for quarter-tone music. Conventional notation and piano techniques can be used, but only half of the pitches are available on each piano or keyboard. The notes must be distributed accordingly. John Eaton's *Microtonal Fantasy* (1966) is played by a single pianist seated in the 90-degree angle formed by the keyboards of two pianos tuned a quarter tone apart. It is recorded on Decca DL710154 along with other Eaton microtonal compositions, which often include a Syn-Ket, an electronic instrument that can be played live before an audience like a conventional instrument.

Ervin M. Wilson has patented a 31-tone keyboard for use in conjunction with the 31-tone scale mentioned previously. The diagram for one octave shown in Example 290 gives some idea of the complexity of the keyboard and the notation. The interval between digitals with successive numbers is 1/31 of an octave. Traditional notation signs are added to letter names in capitals, but in this application double flats and sharps are not enharmonic equivalents of natural notes. Exotic notation signs for the same pitches are added to lowercase letters. Giuseppe Tartini was the source of the fractional flat signs and A. D. Fokker the source of the fractional sharp signs.

Ex. 290 THIRTY-ONE TONE KEYBOARD (Wilson)

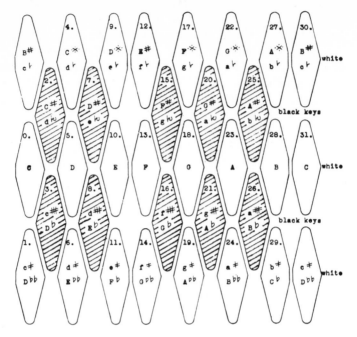

Patent No. 3,012,460. Printed by permission.

The aesthetic value of intervals smaller than a semitone has been studied but not determined. The fact that infinitesimal differences in pitch can be perceived under optimum conditions does not automatically assure their usefulness for artistic purposes. It is unlikely that the smallest perceptible differences in pitch are musically significant, but whether the semitone or some smaller interval represents the ideal minimum is still an open question.

Previously stated problems notwithstanding, the lack of thoroughly compatible systems for notating and performing microtonal and conventional intervals is the most formidable barrier to microtones. Widespread adoption of an incompatible microtonal system would isolate us from our musical heritage and the masterpieces of the past. This, probably more than anything else, gives reason to ponder before yielding to the fascination of microtones.

In spite of the difficulties or perhaps because of them, gifted musicians have labored long on the problems of microtonal music. Occasional performances and record releases attest to their achievements. Musicians who prevail against the years of conditioning to hear any interval smaller than a semitone as out of tune find the best microtonal music genuinely alluring. However, it is still in the pioneering stage, and those attracted to it at this time are more occupied with blazing the trail than with reaping the harvest.

Suggested Assignments

1. Listen to recordings of selected works mentioned in this chapter.
2. Find an example of nonelectronic microtonal music. Identify the source, show the notation, and describe the usage.
3. Prepare a book report on Partch's *Genesis of a Music* or Yasser's *Theory of Evolving Tonality*.
4. Write a short paper outlining the pros and cons of microtonal composition.
5. Practice singing quarter-tone scales. Compare the pitch occasionally with a piano. Alternate notes should match.
6. If you play an instrument capable of producing quarter tones, play a quarter-tone scale up and down between the lowest and highest notes in its normal range.
7. Compose a microtonal exercise for one, two, or three instruments or voices. Adopt one of the notation systems illustrated or devise a new one suited to the specific requirements of your music and medium.
8. Read "Experiments in Notation" by Harry Partch in *Contemporary Composers on Contemporary Music* edited by Elliott Schwartz and Barney Childs (Holt, Rinehart and Winston, 1967).

17

Special Effects

$\mathcal{M}$ANY special effects have been employed concurrently with the basic musical resources and compositional techniques considered in the preceding chapters. The special effect designation in this context denotes the use of unconventional sounds (excluding electronic) requiring special notational devices or performance directions. Each special effect of this type is peculiar to a small group of composers and works, so there is no standardization. Only a few of the infinite possibilities are illustrated. For compendiums of special effects and their notation see the books listed in Suggested Assignment 6 at the end of the chapter.

Special Vocal Effects

Sprechstimme, literally "speaking voice," is a special vocal effect introduced in Humperdinck's 1897 melodrama *Königskinder.* Rhythm and pitch are notated in the conventional way with small X's on the note stems and above or below whole notes signifying *Sprechstimme.* Schoenberg adopted this vocal style initially in *Pierrot Lunaire* and described it in a foreword. The rhythms are executed with no more or less freedom than in ordinary singing. The voice rises or falls from the notated pitch of each note, in contrast to the sustained pitch of normal singing and unlike natural speech.

Ex. 291 SCHOENBERG: *Pierrot Lunaire, No. 7—Der kranke Mond* (1912)

Vocal notation like that in *Pierrot Lunaire* was used almost half a century later by Boulez in *Le Marteau sans Maître.*

Stravinsky wrote a voice part in *Histoire du Soldat* for which only the rhythm is notated. Headless note stems extend down from the third space of a clefless five-line staff. Flags and dots are added to the stems as necessary. Durations longer than a dotted quarter cannot be written, but none are required. There are no sustained tones, and rests complete measures that are not filled by the shorter values. When the voice is silent for a measure or more, the part is omitted from the score. The absence of any pitch notation suggests that the part is to be recited in a monotone or with only normal speech inflections, which is customary in performances. The striking originality of this work is not fully apparent in the concert and recorded versions that include only the instrumental sections of it.

Ex. 292 STRAVINSKY: *Histoire du Soldat* (1918) p1

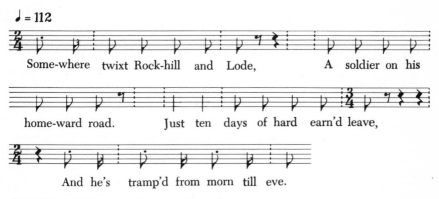

Ligeti exploits the full spectrum of vocal styles in *Nouvelles Aventures* for three singers (coloratura soprano, alto, and baritone), and seven instrumentalists. Booklets which accompany the score give the pronunciation of the phonetic text, transcripts in German and English of the handwritten annotations in the score, and performance instructions. Special instructions for the vocal parts include the following:

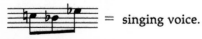 = singing voice.

 = speech-song (*Sprechgesang*) with fixed pitches.

 = speech-song with changing, but not definitely fixed pitches. (The horizontal line corresponds to the middle register of the singer.)

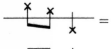 = speaking voice with changing pitch.

 = speaking voice without especially specified pitch (change of pitch *ad lib* but not within too large a range) or with other sounds according to specific instructions in the score.

 = speaking voice, as high as possible (falsetto in baritone).

 = speaking voice, as low as possible.

 = murmuring (*mezza voce*) as high as possible.

= murmuring, as low as possible.

= murmuring, at various pitches.

= unvoiced sounds (whispering).

denotes breathing (unvoiced but very intensive), (▶ = inhaling, ◀ = exhaling).

denotes an inhaling sound: speaking voice simultaneously with inhaling.

The succession of various types of symbols within the same musical phrase does not indicate a sudden change in the kind of execution, but rather a gradual transition.

Ex.: Transition from singing to speech-song and then to speaking voice:

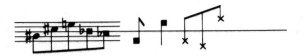

or: gradual withdrawal of the voice (transition from speaking voice to murmuring and then to whispering):

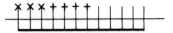

Bar lines serve only as a means of synchronization. They do not indicate stresses and should not be noticeable in performances. In sections designated "senza tempo" the total duration of the section is given in seconds. Within a section the speed of short sounds is relative to the space between note symbols, and the duration of sustained sounds is proportional to the length of the horizontal lines representing them. An excerpt from the score shows several of its special vocal effects and one very special percussion effect.

Ex. 293 LIGETI: *Nouvelles Aventures* (1965) p35

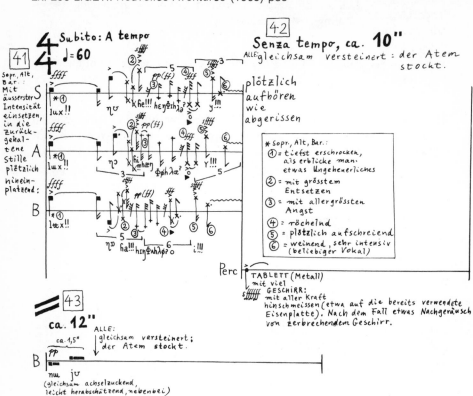

The publisher provides the following English translation of the composer's handwritten annotations in the score.

Bar 41   Soprano, alto, baritone: Enter with the greatest intensity, suddenly bursting into the restrained silence—(1) profoundly shocked, as though at seeing something monstrous; (2) with the greatest horror; (3) with the greatest fear; (4) a rattling in the throat; (5) suddenly crying out; (6) weeping, very intensively (any vowel desired). Stop suddenly as though torn off.

Bar 42   All: As though turned to stone; with bated breath.
Percussion: Metal tray piled high with dishes flung with full force (the iron plate used previously is the best target). The tinkle of breaking china is heard for a moment following the initial crash.

Bar 43   Baritone: As though shrugging, somewhat depreciatingly, offhand.
All: As though turned to stone; with bated breath.

Example 294 shows some of the special effects in the choral parts of Penderecki's *Passion According to St. Luke*. The triangle-shaped symbol indicates the highest note possible (pitch indeterminate), otherwise the placement of the symbols and the direction of the lines following them suggest relative pitch levels. The small circle is the symbol for "mocking laugh."

Ex. 294 PENDERECKI: *Passion According to St. Luke* (1965) p94

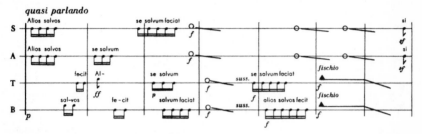

Other special effects Penderecki uses in choral parts include *falsetto* indicated by diamond-shaped note heads, *quasi recitando* indicated by X-shaped note heads, *whispering* indicated by a reversed "S" on headless stems, and *quasi pizzicato* written as beamed groups of stems pointing to various lines and spaces of the staff.

Special Instrumental Effects

Penderecki's *Threnody for the Victims of Hiroshima* contains many special string effects for which the following key to the abbreviations and symbols used in the score serves as a partial catalog. The same quarter-tone symbols are used as in his vocal music (see p. 218).

s. p.	*sul ponticello*—near the bridge
s. t.	*sul tasto*—over the fingerboard
c. l.	*col legno*—with the wood (of the bow)
l. batt.	*legno battuto*—tap with the wood

s. vibr.	*senza vibrato*—without vibrato
gliss.	*glissando*
▲— ↑	highest note on the instrument (indefinite pitch)
↑	play between the bridge and the tailpiece
⫿⫿⫿	*arpeggio*, up or down, over four strings (or those indicated) behind the bridge
┳	play with the bow on the tailpiece
✝	play with the bow on the bridge
𝆑	tap the upper part of the instrument with the nut of the bow or the fingertips
⊓ ∨	change the bow irregularly
∿∿∿	*molto vibrato*
∿∿	very slow *vibrato* with a quarter-tone pitch variation
Ƶ	very rapid, unmeasured *tremolo*
◇	artificial harmonics
⌐	end of an effect

Page 18 of the *Threnody* score, reproduced as Example 295, shows some of its special effects in context. The work is for twenty-four violins, ten violas, ten cellos, and eight double basses, of which all but one viola have a part on the page. Only two of the many different instrument groupings used in the work appear in the excerpt. Each violin in the 1–12 group plays a different pitch in a quarter-tone cluster represented by the solid black band covering the area from G to C above the staff. Unless a staff is required to notate pitches, the parts are written on or as a single line. Where the line is broken or there is no part, the instrument is silent. Time segments marked by vertical dotted lines are numbered consecutively at the top of the score, and the duration in seconds of each segment is shown on a time line at the bottom of the score.

Ex. 295 PENDERECKI: *Threnody for the Victims of Hiroshima* (1960) p18

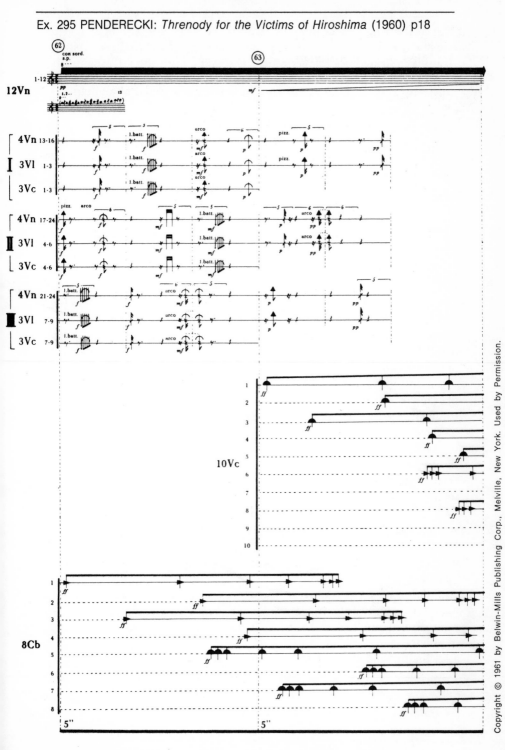

Special string effects in addition to those listed for *Threnody* include two invented by Bartok—*nail pizzicato* and *snap pizzicato*. When nail pizzicato is indicated, the player plucks the string with the fingernail rather than the fleshy part of the finger. The tone quality is more metallic and brittle than that of ordinary pizzicato. To produce snap pizzicato the player plucks the string in a manner that causes it to rebound off the fingerboard with a clearly audible snapping sound. Snap pizzicato figures prominently in the fourth movement of Bartok's *String Quartet No. 4*, and both of these effects are used incidentally in his *String Quartet No. 5*. They are notated as shown.

Nail Pizzicato   Snap Pizzicato

The nature of special effects is such that they usually are peculiar to a particular instrument or family of instruments, but composers have been ingenious in devising new ways of producing sounds on all of them, often by means not normally associated with the instruments. Those listed for the string instruments are typical. The ones found in recent music for other types of instruments are equally varied.

On the piano many special effects are possible beyond the familiar glissandos and the previously discussed tone clusters. Different parts of the instrument, such as the case and the frame, have been used in numerous works as sources of percussive sounds. Henry Cowell was the first to write music that required the strings to be exposed and activated directly rather than by the keys and hammers. He conjures up some strange and wonderful sounds in this manner in his *Banshee* (1925) which can be heard on the *Sounds of New Music* recording (Folkways FX6160). The practice of playing directly on the piano strings is now widespread. They can be activated by plucking, stroking, or striking, and the dampers can be left in place, lifted selectively by depressing the keys, or lifted completely by depressing the sustaining pedal for a wide range of tonal effects.

A different genre of special piano effects is exploited in John Cage's numerous works for "prepared" piano. The preparations, specified for each work, consist of applying such things as screws, bolts, nuts, strips of rubber, and weather-stripping to the strings in ways that drastically alter their sound even when the notation and manner of playing are conventional. *Amores* (1943) is one of several Cage compositions for prepared piano available on disc and tape recordings.

Wind instrument players are sometimes required to hum one pitch while playing another and to produce harmonic intervals, called *multi-phonics*, on their instruments. The possible combinations and method of performance are different for each instrument. At other times no pitch is produced, but the valves or the keys of the instruments are used to make clicking sounds. Almost every instrument has been used at one time or another for percussive effects, and in some avant-garde pieces the instruments are put aside and the players participate in such sound-producing activities as clapping, shuffling their feet on the stage surface, or tapping on the music stand.

Special effects are the stock-in-trade of percussion players. To them have been assigned the parts for everything from anvils to bird whistles, and the list is growing. Automobile brake drums and panels of sheet metal have almost become standard instruments in percussion ensembles. Harry Partch has designed, constructed, and composed music for a whole family of percussion instruments, including several with components salvaged from military bases and antique shops. Special percussion effects can be produced by striking unusual objects and surfaces and by playing ordinary percussion instruments in distinctive ways.

This introduction gives some idea of the vast array of special effects now in use and available to composers. There are many unmentioned, and new ones are being invented every day.

Suggested Assignments

1. Listen to recordings of works or representative excerpts containing special effects.
2. Examine selected contemporary scores to determine which contain special effects as defined in this chapter. Identify the source and give the notation for the special effects you locate.
3. Invent some special effects appropriate for your performing medium and demonstrate them for the class.
4. Explore the possibilities for special effects on the piano using the approaches mentioned in the chapter plus any new ones you can invent. Devise ways to notate those that please you and provide the necessary instructions for potential performers.
5. Compose a piece featuring one or more special effects, or add special effects to augment the color and variety in a piece you have already written.
6. Consult the following books for additional examples of special effects:

Bunger, Richard. *The Well-Prepared Piano.* Colorado Springs: Colorado College Music Press, 1973.

Karkoschka, Erhard. *Notation in New Music.* New York: Praeger, 1972.

Pooler, Frank and Pierce, Brent. *New Choral Notation.* 2d ed., rev. New York: Walton Music Corporation, 1973.

Read, Gardner. *Music Notation.* 2d. ed. Boston: Crescendo Publishing Company, 1969.

7. Listen to *The Piano Music of Henry Cowell,* Folkways record FM3349, on which the composer plays and discusses his many piano styles.

18

Indeterminate Procedures

*T*HE materials and techniques studies thus far have resulted, by and large, from orderly evolutionary processes. The avant-garde styles considered in this and the following chapter, by contrast, have only tenuous connections with historical precedents and depart radically from basic tenets of the past. Revolutionary attitudes currently prevalent in the arts and recent advances in electronic technology, making available extraordinary new sound sources and means of modifying sounds, have impelled music in new directions. Total organization has as its opposite *indeterminate procedures* in which control is relaxed or abdicated, freedom is cultivated, the vagaries of chance and random selection are invoked, and the role of the composer is redefined.

Even the definition of music must be broadened to bring all of the new sound experiences under its mantle. Sounds formerly classified as noise, both electronic and ordinary, are now included regularly in the compositional matrix. In modern parlance only unwanted sounds that interfere with the intended listening are regarded as unmusical. No sound is too bizarre for inclusion in the new music. Prejudices and practical considerations limit the audience for the most extreme styles, but controversy about them generates interest. Young composers intrigued by new resources should not have their natural curiosity stifled. Critics, performers, and listeners, who are sometimes inclined to resist change and to resent the unfamiliar, are reminded that many works now universally recognized as masterpieces were initially decried as radical ventures into cacophonic chaos and appraised as being devoid of musical value.

Improvisation

Improvisation as a word and as a practice has a long and impressive history, but in recent years the term has been applied to music essentially different from its antecedents. Solo improvisation and improvisation from symbols have flourished for centuries. Group improvisation based on a familiar form and harmonic scheme is the mainstay of jazz, but free improvisation by an ensemble breaks with tradition in a fundamental way. The composite sounds that result from free improvisation are not controlled by a single mind or related to a preexistent chord pattern but are basically products of chance. The players may listen critically and attempt to respond appropriately to what they hear in the other parts, but they have no common frame of reference or any way of anticipating what the other players will do at a given moment.

Improvisation as practiced by the Improvisation Chamber Ensemble founded by Lukas Foss in 1957 was not totally free. Preplanning by the members of the ensemble resulted in a specific formal or textural design which was reduced to a chart from which individual parts or *guide-sheets* were extracted. On the charts and guide-sheets any predetermined elements were notated, and the players were assigned such roles as leading, responding, or supporting and such functions as providing the melody (theme), harmony, or counterpoint. The chart for *Music for Clarinet, Percussion and Piano*, Example 296, is representative. The recording of this work (RCA LSC–2558) is out of print, but the Improvisation Chamber Ensemble can still be heard in the improvised interludes of Foss's *Time Cycle* (Columbia CMS–6280). Several other groups have taken up where the Improvisation Chamber Ensemble left off and are cultivating, each in its own way, the art of ensemble improvisation.

Ex. 296 FOSS: *Music for Clarinet, Percussion and Piano* (1961)

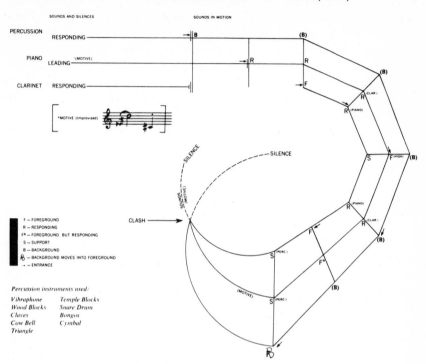

Aleatory

In the type of improvisation described, the performers usurp the composer's prerogatives *in toto* and project their own creativity in their performances. In a related style performers exercise substantial control over the sound events but in compliance with stipulations formulated by the composer. The resulting music is categorized in current terminology as *aleatory* or *aleatoric*, words implying chance or unpredictability. The crux of an aleatoric composition lies in the elements predetermined by the composer and those left to the discretion of the performer. Any aspect of a composition can be fixed or free. For example, pitches can be notated in uniform symbols without rhythmic significance, in which case the performer determines the duration for each pitch; or, durations can be notated without specifying pitches, in which case the performer determines the pitch of each duration. Likewise, tempos, dynamics, articulations, form, and even the medium can be prescribed and the same in all performances or unspecified and potentially different in each realization. The relative degrees of freedom and control vary in existing compositions from almost nil to almost total in both directions. Examples 293, 294, and 295 in the preceding chapter contain aleatoric elements.

An aleatoric procedure which provides a relatively high degree of control over content but permits freedom in organization is for the composer to notate more or less precisely several segments which the performer plays in the order and sometimes in the manner of his choice. Stockhausen's *Klavierstück XI* (1956) is such a piece. It consists of nineteen fragments (distributed over a 37 $\times$ 21 inch area) which the pianist plays in random order as they catch his eye. Six tempos, six dynamic levels, and six articulations are designated from which the pianist elects one combination for each fragment. The piece ends as soon as one of the fragments has been played three times.

The procedures in Stockhausen's *Zyklus for Percussion* (1959) are both similar and different. One player stands in the center of more than twenty percussion instruments arranged in a circle. He turns clockwise or counterclockwise, as he chooses, playing the instruments that come before him during one complete rotation. In place of traditional notation specially conceived symbols are arranged in "time fields" on the sixteen pages of the spiral-bound score, which has no beginning and no end. The player starts wherever he wishes, plays through the remaining pages in order, and completes the cycle by returning to the initial point and repeating the first sound.

Indeterminacy

In general, European composers are more closely identified with the idea of controlled chance or aleatory and American composers with the concept of pure chance or *indeterminacy*. The dividing line between the two categories is not clearly drawn, and the differences tend to be semantic and philosophic rather than technical. John Cage is the high priest and leading exponent of pure chance, and *Indeterminacy* (1959) is the title of a recording (Folkways FT3704) on which he recites ninety disconnected stories, anecdotes, and reminiscences accompanied by material from his *Concert for Piano* (1958) and *Fontana Mix* (1958). A sampling of quotations from the descriptive notes in the Henmar Press catalog of his works gives some idea of his *modus operandi* and provides an introduction to indeterminacy as a trend in new music.

Music for Piano 1 (1952) is written entirely in whole notes, their duration being indeterminate. Each system is seven seconds. Dynamics are given but piano tone production on the keyboard or strings is free. The notes correspond to imperfections in the paper upon which the piece was written. Their number was the result of applying a time limitation to the act of composition itself, changed for each system.

TV Köln (1958) uses noises produced either on the interior of the piano construction or on the exterior, together with auxiliary instruments and keyboard aggregates specified only as to the number of tones in them. The position of notes with respect to lines is ambiguous, referring either to relative pitch, duration, or amplitude.

Imaginary Landscape No. 4 (1951) for 12 radios, 24 players and conductor. The rhythmic structure, 2, 1, 3, is expressed in changing tempi. The notation is in space where ½ inch equals a quarter note. Kilocycle, amplitude and timbre changes are notated. (The sounds are those produced by the radios as the players rotate the tuning, volume, and tone control dials.)

Concert for Piano and Orchestra (1958) is without a master score, but each part is written in detail in a notation where space is relative to time determined by the performer and later altered by a conductor. Both specific directives and specific freedoms are given to each player including the conductor. Notes are of three sizes referring ambiguously to duration or amplitude. As many various uses of the instruments as could be discovered were subjected to the composing means which involved chance operations and the observation of imperfections in the paper upon which the music was written. The pianist's part is a "book" containing 84 different kinds of composition, some, varieties of the same species, others, altogether different. The pianist is free to play any elements of his choice, wholly or in part and in any sequence.

The score of an indeterminate Cage work listed in the catalog and generally known by the duration of its first performance, *4'33"*, is reproduced in its entirety with an appended note as published. The catalog description indicates that the durations were determined by chance operations, but this is not reflected in the score. The only sounds are those incidental to marking the beginning and end of the movements and those occurring spontaneously in the room or concert hall.

Ex. 297 CAGE: *4'33"* (1952)

I

TACET

II

TACET

III

TACET

NOTE: The title of this work is the total length in minutes and seconds of its performance. At Woodstock, N.Y., August 29, 1952, the title was *4'33"* and the three parts were 33", 2'40", and 1'20". It was performed by David Tudor, pianist, who indicated the beginnings of parts by closing, the endings by opening, the keyboard lid. However, the work may be performed by any instrumentalist or combination of instrumentalists and last any length of time.

The sequel to *4'33"*, *4'33"* No. 2 (1962) for which the timing given is 0'00", is a "solo to be performed in any way by anyone." It is also Part 3 of a composite work of which *Atlas Eclipticalis* (1962) is Part 1. The score contains no reference to Part 2, but the catalog indicates the *Atlas Eclipticalis* can also be performed with or without *Winter Music* (1957).

Cage suggests simultaneous performances of some of his indeterminate works, compounding their indeterminacy. His *Aria* (1958), for example, can be performed alone or with *Fontana Mix* or with any parts of *Concert*. There is a recording of *Aria with Fontana Mix*. The version on the recording is, of course, only one of the infinite ways of realizing the two scores. In the notation of *Aria*, time is represented horizontally, pitch vertically, but roughly suggested rather than accurately described. Dotted lines in various colors indicate ten singing styles established by the singer. Black squares are any unmusical uses of the voice or auxiliary devices. The text employs vowels and consonants and words from five languages. Elements which are not notated, such as dynamics, are freely determined by the singer. The score of *Fontana Mix* gives directions for the preparation of any number of tracks of magnetic tape or parts for any number of players of any kind of instruments using a collection of plastic transparencies —ten with variously distributed points, ten with differentiated curved lines, one with a graph, and one with a straight line—which may be superimposed in any number of ways. Example 298 shows one superimposition of the *Fontana Mix* components.

242

Ex. 298 CAGE: *Fontana Mix* (1958)

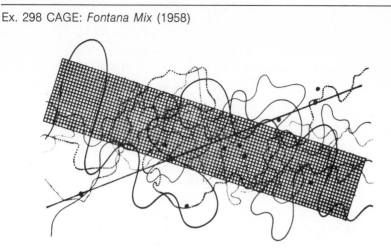

Many composers have been attracted by the possibilities of indeterminacy, Barney Childs among them. His *Intermission Piece* is heard every time players anywhere tune up during an intermission. That *is* the piece. The next step is *conceptual music*, which exists only in the mind. Think of music and it exists, though unwritten and unheard. Nelson Howe's *Fur Music* is an example. He instructs the performer/listener to stroke a fur score and to listen to the music that it produces in his imagination. La Monte Young's *Composition 1960 #10* does not require one even to think of sound but to "Draw a straight line and follow it." Additional examples of this type are described in the chapters on indeterminacy and antimusic in David Cope's *New Directions in Music* (Wm. C. Brown, 1971).

The concepts of music in which performers and listeners become active participants in the creative process, in which constraints are relaxed or abolished, and in which all sounds become grist for the mill open up a bewildering number of tantalizing paths for composers to follow, but they are not without their hazards. Not the least of the hazards is that with the emphasis on freedom, improvisation, and chance the composer's role is reduced from that of the central figure in the musical heirarchy to that of a mere bystander or a thrower of dice. When there is a composer, he does not create compositions in the usual sense but provides raw materials, invents procedures, or describes circumstances which result in performances he might not even recognize. Presumably there is some logical, philosophical, or aesthetic justification for each work, but no discipline can be prescribed for these approaches to composition. They point the way to a whole new realm of creative experiences for performers and listeners. Composers who find them appealing should become acquainted with the field and then follow their own inclinations. For those who do not, there are other directions to go. One of them is *formalized music.*

Formalized Music

The heading of this section is taken directly from the title of the book *Formalized Music: Thought and Mathematics in Composition* (Indiana University Press, 1971) in which Iannis Xenakis describes his revolutionary theories in detail with copious illustrations. His explorations have lead to a sort of abstraction and formalization of compositional processes. He explains in mathematical terms the logical causes of sound sensations and their uses in wanted constructions and attempts to give the art of music a reasoned support less perishable than the impulse of the moment. For his purposes the qualifications "beautiful" and "ugly" are irrelevant. The quantity of intelligence conveyed by the sounds are the true criterion of their validity. He denounces linear thought (polyphony) and perceives contradictions in serial music. In their place he proposes "a world of sound-masses, vast groups of sound-events, clouds, and galaxies governed by new characteristics such as density, degree of order, and rate of change, which require definitions and realizations using probability theory."

Xenakis's approaches to composition can be divided into three related categories: that which uses calculus and the theory of probabilities (*stochastic music*), that which is based on the theory of games (*strategic music*), and that which employs mathematical logic and the theory of sets (*symbolic music*). He utilizes all classes of sonic elements—vocal, instrumental, concrete, (microphone collected), electronic (synthesized), and digital (computer generated). When conventional instruments are the medium, his usual procedure is to represent the mathematical operations graphically and then to transcribe the graphs into staff notation. The graphs of the string glissandos in measures 309–14 of his *Metastasis*, a stochastic composition, are shown in Example 299a. Example 299b includes these same measures in staff notation.

Ex. 299 XENAKIS: *Metastasis* (1954)

a. Bars 309–14

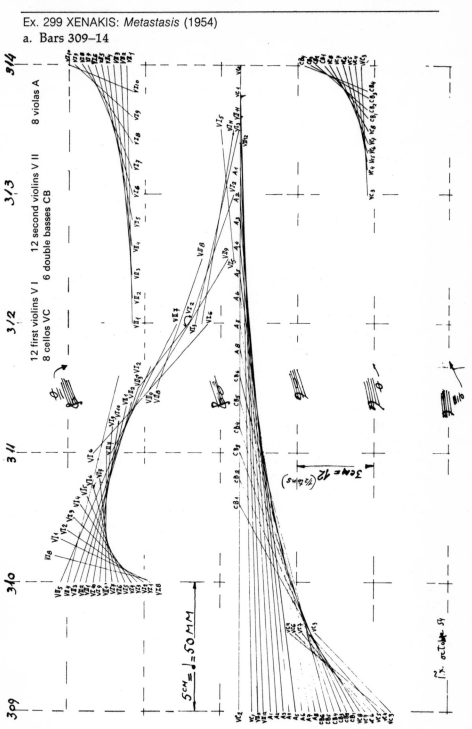

b. Bars 309–17

Xenakis's experiments with *Metastasis* inspired the architectural design of the Philips Pavilion at the Brussels World's Fair where Varèse's *Poème Electronique* was first heard. Xenakis is of the opinion that existing concert halls and amphitheaters are unsuitable for present day music and that a new kind of architecture should be devised. In the meantime he suggests performing works like his symbolic *Terrêtektorh* and *Nomos gamma* in a large ballroom from which all possible aural and visual obstructions have been removed and where the listeners are free to move about or sit on portable stools. The members of the orchestra (90 for *Terrêtektorh* and 98 for *Nomos gamma*) are scattered quasi-stochastically throughout the hall, each seated on an individual dais. This distribution of the players brings a radically new kinetic conception to music and, combined with the mobility of the audience, enriches the compositions in both spatial dimension and movement. Variable speeds and accelerations of sound movement are realized. The composition is thus a "sonotron," to quote Xenakis, "an accelerator of sonorous particles, a disintegrator of sonorous masses, a synthesizer. It puts the sound and the music all around the listener and close up to him. It tears down the psychological and auditive curtain that separates him from the players when positioned far off on a pedestal, itself frequently enough placed inside a box. The orchestral musician rediscovers his responsibility as an artist, as an individual."

The theoretical treatises and compositions of Xenakis exert a profound and growing influence on contemporary musical thought. Their impact would be even greater, no doubt, if more musicians had the necessary command of higher mathematics to comprehend fully his philosophic concepts and to apply his compositional methods.

Suggested Assignments

1. Listen to recordings of works mentioned in the chapter or similar examples illustrating ensemble improvisation and the various approaches to indeterminate music.
2. Prepare an illustrated report on one composer on one aspect of indeterminate music. Demonstration performances or recordings preferably should include different realizations of the same work to highlight the indeterminate elements. Potential composer subjects and sources of information are mentioned in the chapter.
3. Select a small group of performers from the class and experiment with ensemble improvisation.

4. Compose a short work with aleatoric or indeterminate elements and prepare a performance of it for the class.
5. Read "The Changing Composer-Performer Relationship: A Monologue and
a Dialogue" by Lukas Foss in *Perspectives of New Music* 1/2 (Spring 1963)
or the reprint in *Contemporary Composers on Contemporary Music* edited
by Elliott Schwartz and Barney Childs (Holt, Rinehart and Winston, 1967).

19

Electronic and
Other New Music

*A*NY recording or transmission of sound involves electronic equipment, but the designation *electronic music* is reserved for music with sounds modified or generated electronically. Though electronic organs are technically electronic instruments, they were designed as substitutes for conventional instruments and consequently added nothing to compositional resources. The first electronic instruments to produce basically new sounds and to stimulate the composition of distinctive music were the *Theremin*, the *Trautonium*, and the *Ondes Martenot*. All three of these instruments, which stirred musical circles during the 1920s and 1930s, produce an elctronic tone controlled by various manipulations. By 1940 Norman McLaren was making electronic sounds using motion picture equipment. In place of the usual recorded sound track he created images directly on the film by notching the sound area, scratching the emulsion with a stylus, painting dots and other shapes of various sizes on the film, and photographing sequences of cards marked to represent notes. The images passing between an exciter lamp and a photoelectric cell cause current fluctuations that are converted into sound by a loudspeaker. Electronic instruments and the creation of sound on film brought music to the threshold of the electronic age. It arrived with the perfection of the tape recorder.

The tape recorder/player provides not only a highly efficient means of sound recording and reproduction but also several simple and practical ways of modifying sounds. For example, by increasing or decreasing the speed at which the tape travels over the playback head, the pitch is raised or lowered correspondingly. The ends of the tape can be reversed and played backwards, an astonishing effect when the attack and decay patterns are pronounced like those of pianos and percussion instruments. A tape loop fashioned by joining the two ends of a piece of tape repeats a sound pattern endlessly. Sounds can be fragmented and rearranged by cutting and splicing the tape on which they are recorded, and any number of sound tracks can be combined by mixing and rerecording. Starting in 1952 Vladimir Ussachevsky and Otto Luening produced electronic music using tape manipulations of this sort. Ussachevsky's article "The Making of Four Miniatures" in *Electronic Music* (originally published as the November 1968 issue of the *Music Educators Journal*) describes his approach in composing *Four Miniatures*. A sound sheet bound in the book and periodical contains a recording of the work and of the raw materials from which the four pieces were made. Several of his processes can be duplicated with a minimum of equipment and technical know-how. Tape manipulations can, of course, be used on recorded sounds from any source.

Musique Concrete

Electronic music constructed from nonelectronic sounds is called *musique concrete*. Included in the concrete sound category are all sounds both musical and unmusical that come from a vibrating medium. The source may be an instrument, a voice either singing or speaking, or any object or substance that vibrates or can be caused to vibrate in a suitable frequency range. Such seemingly unlikely sources as drops of water, ocean waves, and pinball machines have provided raw material for concrete compositions. The natural sounds are collected by means of microphones and then modified electronically or by tape manipulation.

Pioneering work on concrete music was done by members of the research group organized in 1951 at the Radiodiffusion Française center in Paris, and soon their influence was international in scope. Karlheinz Stockhausen is perhaps the most famous composer of electronic music. His *Mikrophonie I* (1964), which can be heard on Columbia record MS–7355, is a concrete composition for which a tam-tam is the sole sound source. Two microphones were used, according to the composer, "to listen to the tam-tam the way a doctor examines a patient with a stethoscope." Early in his career Stockhausen began using electronically generated sounds. His *Gesang der Jünglinge* (Deutsche Grammophone record DG 138811) completed in 1956 contains, as do many electronic compositions, both concrete and synthesized sounds.

Sound Synthesis

Unlike natural sounds that originate as vibrations, electronically synthesized sounds originate as alternating current signals that can be converted into sound and/or recorded directly on magnetic tape for subsequent conversion to sound. The signals are produced by audio oscillators and generators which, in various combinations and with the proper controls, have the capacity to produce any desired frequency (pitch), amplitude (loudness), and waveform (quality). *White sound* or *white noise* is a distinctive and useful electronic sound that has no specific pitch. Analagous with white light, white sound theoretically contains all of the audible frequencies at random amplitudes. The effect is rather like the hissing sound of escaping steam or the sound of a jet engine. When white sound is filtered, eliminating certain frequency bands, the result is *colored sound.*

The electronic devices used to modify both concrete and electronic sounds include amplifiers, filters, modulators, equalizers, and reverberation units. Processed sounds are recorded on one or more tapes. Multiple tapes are synchronized and their signals passed through a mixer where they are balanced and combined for recording on a final composite tape. The tape recording *is* the work. It may be transferred to discs for commercial distribution, and some graphic representation of its content may be prepared, but the actual composition, in both the general and the specific sense, takes place in the sound studio on the tape. *Poème Electronique* (1958) by Edgard Varèse is, to use the composer's words, an example of "organized sound" created directly on magnetic tape. Oscillator, generator, voice, bell, and percussion instrument sounds, though modified and reshaped, are recognizable in this landmark electronic composition which was first heard through 425 loudspeakers strategically placed throughout the interior of the Philips Pavilion at the Brussels World's Fair.

In the early days of electronic music makeshift devices intended for other functions were used to generate and modify the sound materials. Widespread interest in electronic music and advances in electronic technology led to the development of *synthesizers*, integrated systems of electronic components designed expressly for the production and control of musical sounds, or at least sounds that are used musically, a distinction that is perhaps necessary until electronic instruments gain universal acceptance. The unique RCA Mark II synthesizer acquired by the Columbia-Princeton Electronic Music Center in 1959, the most advanced music synthesizer of its time and still one of the most sophisticated, has the capacity to create any sound that can be adequately specified and emitted by a loudspeaker. Its potential is brilliantly demonstrated in Milton Babbitt's *Ensembles for Synthesizer* (1964). Every parameter of the sound was coded on the punched tape that served as input to the synthesizer. The output signal was not altered after it was recorded nor was the magnetic tape spliced. Babbitt's predilection for conventional pitches and serial organization prevail in the work even though tonal successions sometimes are at speeds too fast for human performance and approaching the limits of perception.

The cost of building the RCA Mark II synthesizer is reported to have been $250,000 or more, and Babbitt is one of the few composers to have mastered its complexities. Where the cost of early prototypes was prohibitive, several standardized makes and models of synthesizers now on the market are in a practical price range for educational institutions and affluent individuals. Capability, versatility, and simplicity of operation are constantly improving, and many colleges and universities now have fully equipped electronic music studios and routinely include the study of electronic composition in the curriculum.

The *Nonesuch Guide to Electronic Music* (stereo album HC–73018) provides an excellent introduction to the sounds, symbols, and terminology of electronic music. The recordings illustrate tones produced by signal generators and the effects of the various control, modulation, and filtering devices commonly available in synthesizers. An enclosed booklet describes basic studio equipment and its functions, proposes a system of notation using diagrammatic symbols, and concludes with a glossary, a bibliography, and the score of a composition realized, as was all of the recorded material in the album, on a Moog Series III synthesizer.

Synthesizers can be and are used to realize scores written in staff notation. The *Nonesuch Guide* and the *Switched-On Bach* recording (Columbia MS–07194) are examples, as are most of the electronic parts in popular music. For most electronic compositions, however, conventional notation is both impractical and superfluous. A preconceived plan, diagram, scheme, or design may be followed in working with the sound materials, but usually there is no score in the ordinary sense. This causes a curious dilemma. In the present outdated and hopefully soon to be revised copyright law, no provision is made for sound recordings. To secure copyright protection for an electronic work in the absence of a score, the composer must transcribe the magnetic tape into some written form. There is no standard system for notating electronic music. Symbols from music and electronics are sometimes used and combined. A method which can be at least partially comprehended by the uninitiated is shown in Example 300.

Ex. 300 ELECTRONIC MUSIC NOTATION

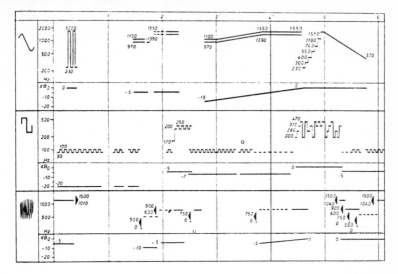

The three symbols on the left in Example 300 represent waveforms and corresponding tone qualities. The symbol at the top is a sine wave, the waveform of a single fundamental frequency without harmonics which is similar in audible effect to a tuning fork or a test tone. More complex waveforms result from combining sine waves of varying frequencies and intensities. Square waves, represented by the symbol in the middle, are produced by combining a fundamental frequency and all odd-numbered harmonics with the intensities of the harmonics inversely related to their frequency. The sound is like that of a clarinet in the chalumeau register. The bottom symbol represents white sound, previously described, from which bands of colored sound are filtered. Pitch and dynamic levels are represented graphically and numerically. The numbers in the top part of each section are frequencies and thus fix the pitches of the sine and square waves and the bands of colored sound. Numbers in the lower part of each section are VU meter readings which establish relative dynamic levels in decibels. Numbers across the top of the score give elapsed time in seconds.

Prerecorded and Live Sound Combined

An obvious disadvantage of pure electronic music is that there is nothing to watch during a performance, a disadvantage shared by all music heard via recordings. The deficiency is remedied in concert performances when live performers are used in conjunction with electronic tapes. Many of the composers who have worked extensively in the electronic medium have explored the possibilities of combining prerecorded and live sound. Live performers supply an intrinsic visual element and at the same time provide a desirable link with more conventional music.

No two works for prerecorded tape and live performers are alike, but *Antiphony IV* by Kenneth Gaburo is representative of the type. It is an intriguing example of new music, because it employs so many of the techniques and materials previously discussed. In addition it exhibits the composer's special interest in *compositional linguistics*, a term he coined meaning, in general, "language as music, and music as language." The work is for piccolo, bass trombone, double bass, and two-channel tape recorder operated by a fourth performer. In a live performance the piccolo and double bass produce normal sounds and many special effects which are amplified but not otherwise modified. The right tape channel consists exclusively of electronically generated sounds: noise bands, high frequency square-wave clusters, low modulated pulse trains, clangorous signals, and percussive synthesized "bass" modulated signals. The left tape channel is composed of vocal sounds derived from a phonetic transcription of a 21-word poem, *Poised*. Phonemes are heard first with the normal voice identity retained and then in progressively more complex electromechanical transformations. *Antiphony IV* is available in a recorded version (Nonesuch 71199) and the complete score is included in Wennerstrom's *Anthology of Twentieth-Century Music* (Appleton, Century, Crofts, 1969). The 21 numbered sections of the score correspond with the 21 words of the poem. Example 301 is section 19, except for a fade-out in the left tape channel, presenting the word "soaring."

In Example 301 the brackets above and below the piccolo (P) line show note groupings; also groups of notes to be played in a particular way, i.e., "breathy" and "N.V." (normal vibrato). The lines terminating in a flat sign indicate that the pitch is to descend a quarter tone from the notated pitch. In the left channel (L) tape notation the X's with dots serving as note heads indicate filtering operations on textual phonemes. Only conventional symbols appear in the bass trombone (T) and double bass (B) parts. In the right channel (R) tape notation the geometric designs represent noise bands; the round symbols linked by curved lines indicate high frequency square-wave clusters; and the pointed symbols depict clangorous signals. Many additional electronic sounds and special instrumental effects are utilized in the other sections of the score.

Ex. 301 GABURO: *Antiphony IV—Poised* (1967)

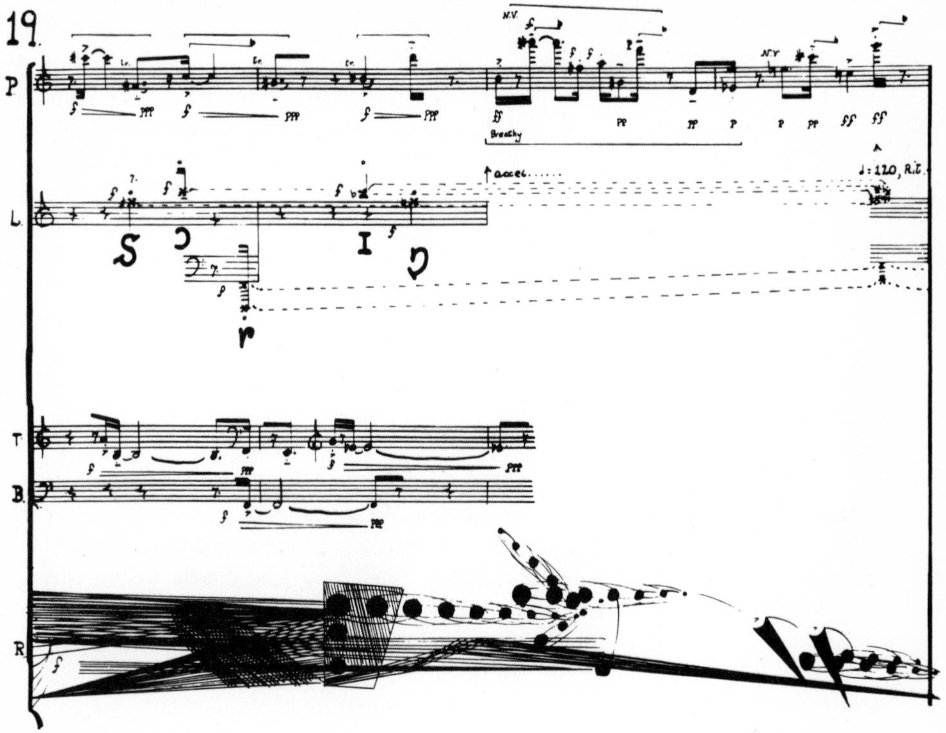

The next step in the evolution of electronic music leads from synthesizers to computers.

Music by Computers

Computer music is still in its infancy. In their 1959 book *Experimental Music* (McGraw-Hill), Hiller and Isaacson could report only six experiments besides their own in which computers had been used to produce music. In the first experiments simple melodies were computer-composed utilizing elementary probability tables for selecting successive notes. Hiller and Isaacson programed a computer to create music consistent with certain technical and stylistic principles. Pitch, duration, dynamics, and playing instructions determined by the computer were represented on a Teletype print-out by numbers, letters, and symbols which were transcribed into conventional notation for live performance. Experiments in this vein using an Illiac computer culminated in their *Illiac Suite* for string quartet. Attempts to link a computer with a Musicwriter for direct production of musical notation were fraught with mechanical problems.

Iannis Xenakis perceived that computers were ideal for executing the long and involved calculations required in the composition of stochastic music. Using FORTRAN IV computer language, he wrote a program for the constituent sequential operations of free stochastic music which is reproduced in his book *Formalized Music* (Indiana University Press, 1971). This program and an IBM–7090 computer were used to produce the data for *Atrées* (1962), *Morisma-Amorisima* (1962), and other of his stochastic compositions. Though the computer print-out for these compositions was converted to staff notation for performance by conventional instruments, he projected the next stage in the development of electronic music—the actual generation of sound by computers.

The modern computer may be regarded as the ultimate electronic music synthesizer. A complete system for the production of computer music requires a digital computer, an appropriate computer program, a digital-to-analog converter, and a loudspeaker. Basically, the characteristics of a sound wave are defined numerically in a language acceptable to the computer, and the sequence of numbers is stored in the computer memory. The numbers in the memory are transferred in succession to a digital-to-analog converter which generates a pulse of voltage corresponding to each number. The resultant pattern of fluctuating voltages smoothed by a filter constitutes an electronic signal that can be recorded on magnetic tape, amplified, and converted into sound by a loudspeaker.

The creation of sound by means of a computer is not as simple as might be presumed from this superficial explanation. Part of the difficulty stems from the innate complexity of the musical sounds that must be represented numerically and the infinite ways they may begin and end. Every parameter of a tone—its pitch, quality, duration, attack, decay, and intensity—must be specified in computer language. Another problem is that for high fidelity sound the numbers from the digital computer must be processed and converted to voltages at the rate of 30,000 or more per second.

A prerequisite for sound synthesis is a very fast and efficient program. Computer programs designed specifically for musical composition have been developed and are being improved constantly. These specialized programs facilitate the encoding of the requisite information and reduce the amount of time and effort the composer must expend on the mechanics of computer programing. Max V. Mathews pioneered sound synthesis by computer at the Bell Telephone Laboratories. His MUSIC IV program and its direct descendant, Princeton University's MUSIC IVB, were designed for use with an IBM 7094 computer. To adapt the MUSIC IV program for the next generation of computers, such as the GE 645, it was rewritten almost entirely in FORTRAN IV and improved, becoming MUSIC V. Part 3 of Mathews's book *The Technology of Computer Music* (MIT Press, 1969) is a MUSIC V manual. In MUSIC V the subprogram "instruments" can play any number of notes at the same time. The program adds and automatically synchronizes all parts and puts out the combined sound. Donald MacInnis has written a music program, MUSIGOL, in Extended ALGOL for computers like the Burroughs 5500 for which that language is particularly appropriate. ORPHEUS, another music program that traces its origins back to MUSIC IV, was written for the CDC–3600 computer at the Argonne National Laboratory. Recorded examples of music produced by this and several other program/computer combinations are included with the book *Music by Computers* (John Wiley and Sons, 1969).

All of the foregoing music programs are based on general-purpose computer languages. To utilize them effectively considerable expertise in computer technology is required, and there is very little carry-over from studies dealing with the traditional symbols of music and the sounds of instruments and voices. Wayne Slawson's article "A Speech-Oriented Synthesizer of Computer Music" in the *Journal of Music Theory* 13/1 (Spring 1969) describes a set of computer programs different in that they utilize synthesized speech sounds and a specification language that can be readily correlated with traditional notation. Those interested in this approach to computer composition, and especially those with access to suitable computer facilities, will want to consult the complete article, but Example 302 will serve as an introduction to the distinctive principles it explores in detail.

The example shows a phrase in ordinary musical notation and as it may be coded for synthesis in a single segment. Event statements in the coded version (the first two columns in the example) are punched on separate IBM cards for computer input. Except when presenting preliminary information, the event statements correspond roughly to notes and rests. "SETUP 2" prepares the preprocessor to accept a two-voice texture, and "MM 108" establishes the tempo or more precisely the pace of the beats, which in this instance are equal to quarter notes. "VOICE 1" and "VOICE 2" identify the two lines in the segment. The phonetic names on the left preceded by periods suggest the character of note-like events—their timbre, attack, release, etc.—for which all acoustic parameters are stored in the computer's memory. The elements in the code following the name are set apart and separated by commas. The first element specifies the pitch by octave, letter name, and chromatic inflection if any. The octaves in the audible frequency range are numbered consecutively from low to high starting from C. Middle C is 5C; the octave below 4C and the octave above 6C. An "S" following a letter name raises the pitch a semitone. Flats are written enharmonically as sharps. An alternate way of specifying pitches is by frequency, which is necessary for pitches outside the tempered scale. The second element indicates duration as a multiple of the beat, using decimals for fractional values. The next two elements are dynamic levels expressed as they would be in musical notation, though they can be specified directly in numbers. When unspecified, the preceding level continues. Additional entries, such as the "A" for accent, follow when they are required. Only the duration is specified for rests. The third column in the example is not part of the code but an interpretation of the second column. Symbols in parentheses are not coded but are implied.

Ex. 302 SLAWSON: *Computer Specification Language*

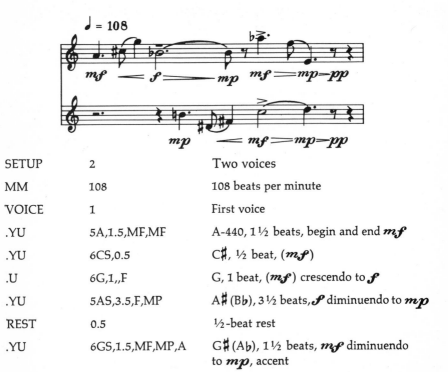

SETUP	2	Two voices
MM	108	108 beats per minute
VOICE	1	First voice
.YU	5A,1.5,MF,MF	A-440, 1½ beats, begin and end *mf*
.YU	6CS,0.5	C♯, ½ beat, (*mf*)
.U	6G,1,,F	G, 1 beat, (*mf*) crescendo to *f*
.YU	5AS,3.5,F,MP	A♯ (B♭), 3½ beats, *f* diminuendo to *mp*
REST	0.5	½-beat rest
.YU	6GS,1.5,MF,MP,A	G♯ (A♭), 1½ beats, *mf* diminuendo to *mp*, accent

258

.YU	6F,0.5,MP	F, ½ beat, *mp*
.U	5E,1.5,,PP	E, 1 ½ beats, (*mp*) diminuendo to *pp*
REST	1.5	1 ½-beat rest
VOICE	2	Second voice
REST	4	4-beat rest
.WI	5B,1.5,MP,MP	B, 1 ½ beats, begin and end *mp*
.WI	5DS,0.5	D♯, ½ beat, (*mp*)
.I	5FS,1,,MF	F♯, 1 beat, (*mp*) crescendo to *mf*
.WI	6C,2,MF,MP,A	C, 2 beats, *mf* diminuendo to *mp*, accent
.I	6D,1.5,MP,PP	D, 1 ½ beats, *mp* diminuendo to *pp*
REST	1.5	1 ½-beat rest
FINISH		End of the phrase

Journal of Music Theory 13 / 1 (Spring 1969). Used by permission.

The recording *Voice of the Computer* (Decca 710180) contains several examples of computer music, including Slawson's *Wishful Thinking About Winter* (1967) which was synthesized using an earlier version of the programs described in his article. J. K. Randall's *Lyric Variations for Violin and Computer* (1967) on Vanguard record VCS–10057 is one of the most ambitious computer compositions to date. It was synthesized using a MUSIC IVB program and an IBM 7094 computer. Recordings of computer compositions are listed in the "Electronic Music" section of the *Schwann Record & Tape Guide.*

Development of the first full-fledged special-purpose computer language for music, TEMPO (Transformational Electronic Music Process Organizer), was started by John L. Clough and his associates at Oberlin College in 1968 and subsequently continued at the University of Michigan where the language was initially implemented. An adjunct program, PLAY, controls the digital-to-analog conversion process. A special feature of the system is MUTILS, a set of routines for real-time sound synthesis, that is, a one-to-one ratio between computer time and sound output. The great advantage of real-time synthesis is that the sound can be monitored as it is generated by the computer, eliminating the customary delay imposed by the high sampling rate required for high fidelity sound.

A promising new way of describing sound sequences to computers is to represent them graphically using a light pen to draw on a cathode ray tube (CRT) attached to a small computer. The small computer reads the graphs and transmits the information digitally to a larger computer, after which the synthesizing process is the same as for other input modes.

The full range of audible frequencies is available in computer music, but the pitches can be limited to those of conventional scales, a twelve-tone scale, or any arbitrary set of pitch relationships. Computers can be programed to produce strict serial music or to make random selections within prescribed limits and in a sense to "compose" in accordance with instructions provided by the programer. Computer music in which a significant portion of the compositional decisions are made by the computer is another type of indeterminate music. A computer controlled by a program which defines general extents rather than details and directs random selection for unspecified parameters of sound will produce many variants of the same composition.

The exploration of the computer's potential as a musical instrument has just begun. Present limitations are more in the operators than in the machines. Scientists skilled in computer technology are rarely disciplined in the art of music, and comparatively few composers have sufficient knowledge of mathematics, acoustics, and programing to cope effectively with the complexities of modern computers. These deficiences are apparent in some of the early music by computers, but at the present rate of development computer music a few years hence will make that of its first decade seem primitive by comparison. The ultimate applications of electronic technology to music probably will not have been reached until works composed and synthesized by computers, recorded on tape, and played through loudspeakers are reviewed by robot critics for other robots who did not make it to the concert.

Multimedia

Multimedia and *mixed media* are terms applied to contemporary works in which two or more distinct art forms are combined. Technically, a composite art form such as opera or ballet qualifies for the category, but in current usage the terms generally imply a combination of avant-garde music with spectacular visual effects. The visual elements may be supplied by live musicians, actors, or dancers; they may be still or moving projected images or merely a display of lights within the hall, a so-called *light show*. Senses other than hearing and sight may be involved and sensory stimulation outside the performance area regarded as relevant to the artistic experience. Aleatory is the rule rather than the exception. When significant elements of the production are left entirely to chance, the result is a *happening*. Audience participation is often encouraged. More extreme multimedia concepts lead to *total theater* in which distinctions between composer, performer, and spectator are obscured. Philosophically and aesthetically the multimedia protagonists are heading in a direction that ultimately leads to embracing all sensual experience as art and in which distinctions between art and life approach the vanishing point.

The styles and techniques of new music have been surveyed. Which of them, if any, will survive and flow into the mainstreams of the future? Which will fade into oblivion? Will the next trend be a revival from the past or a totally new discovery? Only time will tell, but musicians contribute to the eventual decisions every time they write, play, sing, or listen to a piece of music.

Suggested Assignments

1. Listen to recordings of the works cited in this chapter or similar examples illustrating the various types of electronic music.
2. Prepare a report on some phase of electronic music and illustrate it with appropriate recordings. Potential sources of information in addition to those mentioned in the chapter are biographical entries for composers active in the styles, program notes for records and concerts of new music, and the following article and books:

Clough, John. "TEMPO: A Composer's Programming Language." *Perspectives of New Music* 9/1 (1970): 113–125.

Cope, David. *New Directions in Music.* Dubuque: Wm. C. Brown Company Publishers, 1971.

Ernest, David. *Musique Concrete.* Boston: Crescendo Publishing Company 1972.

Lincoln, Harry B., ed. *The Computer and Music.* Ithaca: Cornell University Press, 1970.

Sear, Walter. *The New World of Electronic Music.* New York: Alfred Publishing Company, 1972.

Strange, Allen. *Electronic Music.* Dubuque: Wm. C. Brown Company Publishers, 1972.

3. Analyze and write a summary of the procedures in a particular work in which prerecorded and live sound are combined.

4. Attend a multimedia concert or a musical happening.
5. Make a tape illustrating effects that are possible with concrete sounds and simple tape manipulations.
6. Using available facilities, experiment with electronic sound generation and control and assemble the results in a logical sequence.

20

Practical Suggestions

$\mathcal{A}$ common question is whether or not a piano should be used in writing music. The only answer is that each individual must discover for himself the best approach, and it is not the same for every type and phase of composition. An instrument is little help in conceiving and notating rhythms and may be unnecessary in writing melodies, but a piano is indispensable for those not endowed with extraordinary aural powers when exploring and testing complex harmonic progressions.

There are certain dangers in relying too heavily on an instrument. One is that it fosters the habit of improvising rather than composing, and many good ideas no doubt have been lost as a result. Another danger especially applicable to pianists is that they tend to write finger patterns rather than anything truly creative. Also, those who write with an instrument tend to dissipate valuable time playing a progression or melody over and over before writing it, and the final version may be no better than the first. Effective revision is more likely after the ideas are down in black and white.

On the other side of the ledger, interesting sonorities and idiomatic figurations have resulted from chance discoveries at the keyboard, and wrong notes and faulty progressions have been found and corrected with the aid of a piano. Whether one writes everything or nothing at the piano or uses a compromise system, he has good company in the ranks of distinguished composers, for among them methods ranging from one extreme to the other are used successfully.

The assistance of a piano is precluded in some advanced styles and minimal in others. Microtones cannot be played on a piano, and a piano is useless in executing a plan of total organization or in projecting the outcome of indeterminate procedures. For the latter it is knowing the psychology of performers—being able to attract their attention, to motivate them, and to anticipate their reactions—that is important. As for electronic music, the composer's primary concern in the early stages is becoming familiar with the equipment, and the next stage is usually one of trial and error.

Electronic composers are not ordinarily concerned with notation, but for others the ability to write legible music manuscript is a prime requisite. This skill is acquired mainly by practice, but many shortcuts can be learned from an experienced copyist. Just observing an expert at work is instructive. Having the proper equipment and supplies is also a great asset. They can be purchased in the places that specialize in music reproduction and, except for paper, in most art supply stores and college bookstores.

Blank music paper is available in a wide range of sizes and styles suitable for all usual requirements. Sketching is done in soft (No. 1 or 2) pencil, but black ink should be used for finished copies. Pelikan Fount India, Artone Fountain Pen India, and Higgins Eternal carbon inks produce copy that is easy to read, even when illumination is less than perfect, and which reproduces well by all duplicating processes. Ordinary fountain pen inks tend to smudge (though this can be prevented by spraying with Krylon Workable Fixatif), and they are not sufficiently dense for reproduction by some processes. A preliminary pencil copy can be "inked in" to provide an ink copy with the least risk of copying errors. Since some corrections are inevitable, a Mercury electric eraser is a marvelous time-saver.

Pens used for music copying ideally should be capable of producing all of the music symbols with minimum effort and maximum speed. Note heads and beams must be broad, and note stems and bar lines must be relatively thin. In general the point should make broad horizontal lines and narrow vertical lines when the angle and pressure of application are proper. Some copyists prefer a point that will spread to fill a staff space with a solid note head in one stroke. Others prefer a narrower point and use a circular motion for solid note heads. Open note heads are made with a larger circular motion or by two strokes from left to right. Note heads should be the full size of the space between staff lines. This is especially important in instrumentral parts which must be read from a distance. To draw straight bar lines without smearing, use a draftsman's lining pen and a ruler with a raised edge.

The least expensive pens suitable for music copying consist of a steel nib such as an Esterbrook No. 442 Jackson Stub inserted in a wooden holder with a cork grip. They are light and comfortable in the hand but require frequent dipping, a problem that can be alleviated by adding to the nib an Inkspoon of the type manufactured by H. Mauri & Company. Holding a new nib over a lighted match for a few seconds and then dipping it in ink while still hot improves its performance.

Several companies make fountain pens suitable for music copying. Waterman makes a special three-prong music point which is broad and smooth and especially good for copying parts. Platignum pens come with six interchangeable points. Ozmiroid Italic Oblique points, available in fine, medium, and broad, are well suited to music copying requirements, and they fit in both Ozmiroid and Esterbrook barrels. Some copyists shape Esterbrook points to their individual requirements by filing. Faber-Castell 5564B pens have the special advantage of a cap that prevents the ink from drying and clogging the point.

Correct notation facilitates reading and impresses performers, conductors, and publishers, yet few musicians are adequately instructed in its details. Carl A. Rosenthal's *Practical Guide to Music Notation* (MCA Music, 1967) is highly recommended as a reference, and the inexpensive booklet *Standard Music Engraving Practice* prepared by the Music Publishers Association and published by the Music Educators National Conference answers the common questions about notation. Improper alignment is a frequent source of difficulty in performing and analyzing manuscript music. Notes which sound simultaneously must be exactly aligned on the score.

Scores and parts for orchestral and chamber music must be prepared meticulously to conserve rehearsal time, which is always at a premium. Preferably every note should be checked to eliminate errors, but at least the measures in each part should be counted to avoid wasting rehearsal time tracking down omitted measures and miscounted rests. The complexity and unfamiliarity of new works causes much starting and stopping in rehearsals, so the measures should be numbered or a rehearsal number or letter given every few measures.

Multiple copies of scores and parts are frequently required. The Ozalid process is generally most economical and satisfactory for reproducing limited quantities. The original copy is made on transparent onionskin paper using a pen and dense ink. The writing is done on the opposite side from the lines so that erasures leave the lines intact. Some composers score directly on onionskin paper to avoid recopying. Typewriting will reproduce on Ozalid machines if it is done with a carbon ribbon or with carbon paper backing the original. Transparent masters can be made from opaque originals, but this increases the cost. Companies that specialize in Ozalid music reproduction ordinarily provide while-you-wait printing and binding and prompt mail service to outlying areas. They carry a full line of onionskin paper and music copying supplies.

Xerox machines have revolutionized the copying industry, but they were not designed for music. They print on only one side of the paper; the popular letter and legal sizes are narrower (8½ inches) than standard music papers; and the centers of solid note heads are sometimes faded on the prints. If the print quality and size problems can be solved, the single pages can be pasted back to back or taped together for accordion folding. Photo-offset printing is the best and least expensive for the large quantities required for commercial distribution and some choral works, though the initial cost is relatively high. Ditto and Mimeograph machines are used for duplicating classroom music materials, but the other duplicating processes are preferable for scores and parts.

Musicwriters, similar to typewriters, have been on the market for several years. They are capable of producing music copy comparable in appearance to published music, but few composers are willing to invest the money in the machine or the time in the copying to achieve that degree of perfection. Some hand finishing is required on Musicwriter copy, and the whole operation is much slower than writing ordinary hand manuscript, which is adequate for most purposes.

When a composer has a work written and copied, his next problem is finding performers. The task is not always easy, but the barriers are not insurmountable if the goals are realistic. Players, singers, and conductors are becoming more receptive to new works. High school, college, and university musical organizations are an attractive outlet. Friends and acquaintances can be induced to include new compositions on their recitals. Competitions and commissions are an added incentive to write, and performances of successful works are assured. Securing performances and recognition are second only to the composing itself in determining a composer's career.

The choice of medium and the degree of difficulty are critical factors in getting performances. Works written especially for friends, with their capabilities and limitations in mind, are certain to be appreciated. Compositions for instruments or ensembles for which the literature is sparse are more apt to receive a favorable reception than string quartets and symphonies. Works compatible with the tastes, technique, and instrumentation of amateur groups will be performed sooner and more often than those geared to professional standards. These suggestions point to solo instruments (preferably played by friends), less usual chamber music combinations, and band as the logical mediums for composers seeking recognition. An alternative is electronic composition, which bypasses the whole problem of performance except in the sense of finding audiences to listen to the tapes.

Few aspiring composers are sufficiently optimistic to anticipate making a living from their works, but seeing them in print is not too much to hope for. Though the popular music field is practically closed to outsiders and manuscripts are returned unopened, prospects in some other areas are more favorable. The most promising field for composers who aspire to be published is in music for the mass market of the public schools. The Selective Music Lists compiled for music educators are comprised primarily of recent compositions and arrangements, and publishers are always looking for suitable new works. Difficulty and style are restricted, which discourages many composers, but writing for this market is a tremendous challenge and opportunity. The prevalence of conservative and unimaginative pieces on student recital and concert programs is due, at least in part, to a shortage of more adventuresome works in the proper grade levels. To rectify this situation, composers must take the initiative. School age is not too soon to expose the younger generation of musicians and music lovers to the riches of the contemporary musical language.

Since the uninitiated are understandably dazzled and bewildered by modern music's complexities and anachronisms, musicians must become familiar with its materials, procedures, and literature to prevent the decline of serious music into an esoteric art practiced by and accessible to only devotees and antiquarians. The dramatic innovations in the music of this century have only kept pace with the advances in science and technology and with the changes in the other arts, in our attitudes, and in our social institutions. The music of our time, like that of any time, can be no more nor less than a reflection of the society and the individuals that produce it. The music of any moment is not merely a transient episode but the culmination of the past and the foundation of the future, which always meet in the present. This book will have achieved its purpose to the extent that it illuminates these concepts and contributes to the understanding and command of the TECHNIQUES OF TWENTIETH CENTURY COMPOSITION.

Digest of Musical Forms

The study of composition is not complete without some consideration of the ways melodic, rhythmic, and harmonic resources are organized into complete works, though a detailed study of form in twentieth-century music is beyond the scope of this volume. The following digest is intended as an introduction, a review, or a supplement—depending upon individual circumstances—of traditional forms with some comment on contemporary applications.

Part Forms

The simplest musical form consists of a single musical idea. It is characterized by a high degree of unity since contrasting ideas are lacking. It has but one complete cadence which concludes the piece. The idea may be repeated, literally or varied. Many folk and familiar songs and hymns have a one-part melody which is repeated with each verse of the text. The length of individual musical ideas varies considerably, but pieces with only one are limited in extent. Contemporary one-part forms are found mostly in folk song settings and teaching pieces. Internal structures of contemporary musical periods (also called sentences), which are similar to one-part forms, are illustrated in Chapter 2. Though these examples are taken from larger works, they illustrate the usual internal structures of single ideas. Observe that repeated elements often occur within a period.

Forms are extended by a cumulative process. After the one-part form is a two-part or *binary* form. This is the form traditional for movements of baroque suites and partitas. In these works the first part starts in the tonic key and modulates to a related key, most often the dominant, where it cadences. The second part starts in the related key, modulates back to and ends in the tonic key. Each part is repeated, so the complete form is represented schematically by the letters AA BB. The two parts may be approximately the same length, or the second may be longer. The same thematic material is used in both, but it is transposed and may be modified by inversion and similar devices. The change of tonality is the main source of variety. Unifying elements are stressed, and consistency of style, tempo, and mood is maintained.

Since only limited contrast is logically possible in the two-part format, three-part or *ternary* designs have been in greater favor since the baroque era. Essentially, a ternary form consists of a statement of a thematic idea, a departure, and a return. The form is represented schematically by the letters A B A. Within this basic framework, infinite variety is possible.

The A period may be all in one key, modulate and return, or modulate and cadence in the new key. The B section may be just a bridge passage between A and its return, or it may be a phrase, a period, a group of phrases, or a developmental section based on A material. Some degree of contrast is essential, and a change of tonality is expected. The return of A may be literal, modified, abridged, or extended. If the initial A cadences in a key other than tonic, its return is altered to end in the tonic key.

The parts of ternary forms frequently are repeated. The repetition of the first part only produces the AA B A pattern typical of popular songs. Classic and romantic ternary forms often have a pattern of repetition which stems from the binary concept. The first part is repeated, and the second and third parts are repeated together, AA BA BA. Other patterns of repetition are comparatively rare. Contemporary composers are inclined to eliminate or modify repetitions. Examples of ternary form abound in all styles as short, independent pieces and as parts of larger works.

Ternary forms sometimes conclude with a *coda*. A coda is a passage beyond the basic design of the form which normally follows a cadence, real or implied, in the main tonality. A coda serves to bring the piece to a more complete and satisfying close. Codas are proportioned to the rest of the work. Those attached to simple ternary forms are brief, but it is not uncommon for larger forms to have extended, multisectional, developmental codas.

Binary and ternary forms are combined to make more extended compositions. The usual *march form* is a large binary or *compound binary* with the march proper as the first part and the trio as the second part. The march and the trio individually have simple binary or ternary structures with the usual repetitions. The trio begins and ends in a related key, usually the subdominant. Since the trio concludes the work, there is no return to the tonic key. March form is the only one in current use which regularly ends in a different key than it begins.

Marches and most other forms may begin with an *introduction*. An introduction is any passage which precedes the main body of the composition. Introductions establish the tonality and mood of the piece and set the stage for the entry of the main thematic material. They range in length and importance from a few beats of accompaniment figure to extended passages with thematic significance.

Except for marches, a far more common form is large or *compound ternary*. This is the form used for minuets, scherzos, and da capo arias. *Minuet and trio* form is another name for it. It consists of three parts, of which the third is a repetition of the first. Each part is in itself a small form, usually ternary. Typically the third part is a literal return of the first, minus repeats, indicated by a da capo at the end of the second part. Since repeat signs are ignored in the da capo, the third part is of shorter duration than the first. In current composition extended literal repetitions are so rare that the da capo sign has all but disappeared from musical notation. Codas are fairly common in compound ternary forms, but introductions are rare.

A similar form with two trios separated by an additional return of the opening material is also encountered occasionally.

Rondo Forms

The principle of alternation is embodied in *rondo* forms. A fixed thematic element usually called a *rondo theme* alternates with subsidiary thematic elements. These subsidiary thematic elements are referred to variously as *subordinate themes*, *episodes*, or *digressions*. As in so many aspects of music, there is no common terminology. There is not even complete agreement on what constitutes a rondo.

The early examples have many parts each a period in length with little or no transitional material between them. The rondo theme is always in the tonic key with its appearances separated by contrasting sections in different keys. The *Gavotte en Rondeau* from Bach's *E Major Partita* for solo violin is a well known example of this type. It has nine parts with an A B A C A D A E A design.

In subsequent applications of the rondo principle the tendency has been to reduce the number of parts to five or seven and to increase their size. Individual parts may be binary or ternary as well as one-part forms. Transitional material and modulatory passages introduced between themes of rondo forms give them a degree of continuity and unity which distinguishes them from sectional part forms. Stressing continuity, unity, and the use of transitions as decisive characteristics, some theorists classify large A B A designs which have them as rondos. Whether this form, which is common for slow movements, is more properly classified as a rondo or as a large ternary is an academic question.

The rondo principle of thematic alternation becomes apparent when three appearances of the rondo theme are separated by two contrasting sections in an A B A C A pattern. Each section may be a one-part, binary, or ternary form. Transitions between sections are typical as is a coda after the third appearance of the rondo theme.

The most prevalent rondo form is achieved by bringing back the first contrasting section transposed to tonic and an additional return of the rondo theme beyond the five-part plan outlined above. This gives an A B A C A B' A design. The transposition of a subsidiary theme to the tonic key relates this type of rondo form to sonata form. When the C section is developmental as it sometimes is, rather than a new theme, the relationship is even closer. Rondos with seven parts are inclined toward a three part balance, ABA C AB'A, with the middle part, C, longer than the other individual parts. The C section usually is a multipart form extended by repetitions or a multisectional development of previously stated themes.

To avoid monotony the rondo theme is modified and/or abbreviated in some of its appearances. One may even be missing. The final return of the rondo theme is the one most often omitted, and this requirement of the form is then satisfied by references to the theme in the coda. In other words, the final statement of the rondo theme is merged with the coda. The coda then is apt to be an elaborate developmental section, sometimes with references to other thematic elements as well as to the rondo theme. Mozart modified a basic seven-part rondo design by suppressing the usual statement of the rondo theme between the C and B' sections, thus ABA C —B'A. In modifications such as these, contemporary composers have been particularly imaginative.

The themes of rondo forms do not have to bear the weight of a development section except in the one hybrid type. The rondo and subsidiary themes typically have a straightforward songlike or dancelike quality. Between the main structural units of a rondo almost anything is possible. The close of one section may be followed immediately by the beginning of the next. More often a transition intervenes. The transition may be a simple modulatory passage which takes the most direct route to the required tonality, or it may rival the themes in extent and substance. A cohesive structure is achieved by building the transitions out of thematic material, but composers sometimes prefer to provide performers with brillant passage-work for technical display at these points.

Rondo form is used for independent pieces but is more common in the finales of symphonies, sonatas, concertos, and comparable works.

Sonata Form

The tripartite concept is extended to major proportions in *sonata* form. The exposition, development, and recapitulation are three main structural divisions of approximately equal length. The material of the exposition returns with codified modifications in the recapitulation.

An introduction frequently precedes the exposition proper. It may be merely a brief passage leading to the announcement of the first theme, or it may have an extensive sectional structure. It may introduce elements of thematic significance, foreshadow future themes, or be an independent section without thematic relationship to the rest of the movement. A contrasting slow tempo normally sets the introduction apart from the exposition of fast movements in sonata form. Slow movements in the form rarely have introductions.

The exposition presents all of the thematic material, customarily with three divisions designated principal theme, subordinate theme, and closing group or first theme, second theme, and third theme. Each theme may vary in length and structure from one period to several parts depending upon the scope of the movement. The principal theme is stated entirely in the tonic key in tonal compositions. The statement presents the elements of the theme in a concise fashion. Good sonata themes contain motives which are available for future development, but most of the elaboration is reserved for the development section and the coda. Contrast between the themes is essential to the modern concept of sonata form. The means of achieving the contrast, whether by changes in tonality, mood, tempo, or style varies with the period, the composer, and the work. The first theme is usually the more dramatic and energetic of the three, though exceptions occur.

The statement of the principal theme is followed by a passage of varying length and importance which leads to the mood, tempo, and tonality of the second or subordinate theme.

In tonal works the subordinate theme is in a related key, usually the dominant or relative major or minor. Contemporary examples of the form favor more remote relationships. In styles where tonality is obscure, other contrasting factors compensate. Traditionally the second theme is lyric in quality, contrasting with the first.

272

In early examples of the form the third or closing theme is little more than a cadential passage. Later it assumes full thematic stature, often with several distinctive motives some of which may be derived from previous themes. Fragmentary treatment is more likely in the closing section than in the statements of the first and second themes. The closing theme, which originally grew out of the second, may continue in the same tonality and mood of the preceding section, but the trend is toward greater individuality and autonomy.

The closing theme completes the exposition with a definite cadence in a tonality other than the tonic. In classic sonata forms the exposition is repeated. The double bar appearing in some contemporary works at this point is a vestigial remainder of the repeat sign. The repeat sign, where it occurs, is often ignored in current performances. Reflecting the disdain with which literal repetition is now regarded, twentieth-century composers practically never write it.

The skill and imagination of the composer are unfettered in the development section. Every manipulation and combination of any and all themes is invited. The introduction of new material does not violate the concept of the form, though it is superfluous when the themes have been well selected and constructed. The structure of the development is sectional. It builds up to one of the main climaxes of the movement and usually has other, secondary climax points. Remote tonalities are explored even in classic compositions. Only the tonic, which would anticipate the recapitulation, is avoided. The development may end and the principal theme make its reentrance with a climax, or the climax in the development may subside prior to a quiet return of the first theme.

The beginning of the recapitulation is heralded by the return to the tonic tonality and an easily recognized version of the principal theme. Early users of the form were content to make the recapitulation virtually a repetition of the exposition with only the necessary changes in the transitions and the required transposition of the subordinate and closing themes. The prescribed key for all themes in the recapitulation is tonic. Departures from the tonic key may occur in the episodes between themes. The inherent problem of tonal monotony in the traditional recapitulation plan has been resolved by composers in various ways. In twentieth-century sonata forms where tonality is not decisive as a structural element, unity and variety are obtained by other means, and typical freedom is exercised in the tonality of the themes in the recapitulation as elsewhere.

The recapitulation completes the basic sonata form, but more often than not it is followed by a coda. The coda may be no more than a brief cadential passage which serves to bring the movement to a close, but it may have an extended sectional structure and amount practically to a second development section. The coda may use material from any of the themes and introduce new ideas as well. The recall of elements from the introduction is an effective unifying device. Extended codas frequently have the biggest climax of the movement, but they also may lead to quiet endings. Finding just the right conclusion for a movement is one of the arts of composition.

Quite a few early examples of sonata form indicate a repetition of the development and recapitulation together. This reflects the pattern of repetition associated with simple ternary form in which the first part is repeated and the second and third parts are repeated together. Conductors and performers no longer observe repeat signs at the end of movements in sonata form, and composers have long since ceased to write them. That the same pattern of repetition exists at all in simple ternary and extended sonata forms is an indication of the underlying relationship between them.

The foregoing summarizes the general characteristics of sonata form. An examination of specific works will reveal infinite variation of detail within this broad outline.

Sonata form, with its ternary implication, has a binary counterpart —*abridged sonata* or *sonatina* form. This form has all the features of sonata form except the development. The exposition is followed immediately or after a bridge passage by the recapitulation. In the absence of a development section the coda sometimes assumes added importance and in a sense becomes a development section though it retains its position following the recapitulation.

A modified sonata form with a double exposition is customary for first movements of concertos. The first exposition in the orchestra is all in the tonic key. The solo participates in the second exposition which has the usual sonata form key relationships. The cadenza, when there is one, normally comes after a tonic six-four chord in the tonic key between the recapitulation and the coda.

The form diagramed in the section on rondo forms exhibiting certain sonata form characteristics (ABA C AB'A) is a sort of hybrid. Generally classified as rondos, these hybrids are variously known as *rondo-sonatas, sonata-rondos,* or simply as a type of rondo. They have alternate repetitions of a theme, like rondo forms, and a return of the second theme transposed to the tonic key, like sonata forms. The fourth of their seven parts may be a new theme or a development section. Those with a new theme are more akin to rondo form; those with a development section are closer to sonata form.

274

Contrapuntal Forms

The forms previously considered sometimes are lumped together as homophonic forms as distinguished from the contrapuntal forms. The fundamental difference stems from the manner of repetition. Homophonic forms are achieved by alternate repetition, that is, the reappearance of themes after a departure, while the contrapuntal forms are achieved primarily by immediate repetition in another voice.

Repetition in a *canon* is continuous. A line started in one part is imitated a few beats or measures later in one or more other parts. The imitation may be at the unison or any interval. The end of *round canons* or *rounds* leads back to the beginning, so they can be repeated infinitely. Others break the imitation at the end to make a cadence. Canons with the imitation in inversion, retrograde, retrograde inversion, augmentation, and diminution are possible. Canons may be accompanied by free voices. Despite some notable exceptions, the strict imitation of the canon limits its usefulness as an independent form. Its principal function is in passages of works with some other overall structure.

Fugue, on the other hand, is a form admirably suited to complete works in a wide variety of styles. It starts with the statement of a concise theme, called a *subject,* in one voice alone. The subject is then stated in succession by each of the other voices of the fugue, most often three or four. As each completes its statement of the subject, it continues with a counterpoint to the subsequent subject appearance. When one counterpoint is systematically associated with the subject, it assumes thematic significance and is known as a *countersubject.* The main exposition of the fugue is complete when each voice has stated the subject. Sometimes there is an extra subject entrance in the exposition or a counterexposition, in which each voice has the subject a second time.

Traditionally the second statement of the subject is in a dominant relationship to the first. This version is called the *answer.* It is *real* if the intervals are identical with the subject; *tonal* if they are altered at the beginning to remain temporarily in the tonality of the subject. Modern composers favor real answers, and answers at intervals other than the fourth and fifth are common.

The main exposition is followed by a series of entrances of the subject in various voices and keys. In this section all sorts of manipulations and combinations of the subject and countersubject are exploited. Passages of free counterpoint, usually employing motives from the subject or countersubject, intervene between thematic entrances. The return to the tonic key characteristically is associated with an overlapping or *stretto* of subject entrances which concludes the form.

Fugal expositions and fuguelike passages called *fugatos* frequently are incorporated in other forms, especially in the development sections of sonata forms.

Variation Forms

The variation principle consists of the continuous repetition of one or more thematic elements while the others are varied. Historically, variations are classified according to the particular element repeated.

Chorale preludes, which are a type of variation, use the chorale melody as the basis of the variations. The melody is embellished, provided with enriched settings, or its phrases used imitatively in the variations.

In *chaconnes* and *passacaglias* a bass line or a harmonic progression, traditionally eight measures long, is repeated continuously as the basis for a series of variations. *Grounds* and *ostinatos* are constructed similarly, but the repeated element is shorter.

Classic *theme and variations* have a one-part, binary, or ternary theme, often with one of the repeat patterns associated with the part form. The melody of the theme and/or the harmonies which accompany it serve as the basis for the variations, and the original structure of the theme with any distinctive modulations, cadences, and repetitions is retained. Since the closed form of the theme ends with a complete cadence, each variation does also. This produces a break between variations and sectional divisions in contrast to the continuity exemplified in chaconnes and passacaglias.

Free variations are a more recent type. In free variations a theme is used as a point of departure, but beyond that no procedures are prescribed. A motive may be extracted from the theme to provide the only thematic reference in an entire variation. The melodic, harmonic, and rhythmic material may be new and the form of individual variations different from each other and from the theme. When all of the elements are subject to variation, careful analysis is sometimes necessary to reveal the tenuous relationship between the theme and the variations. The variation techniques employed in free variations are not peculiar to the variation forms. They are found in the developmental passages of all forms.

Sectional variations do not lend themselves to the building of monumental climaxes. This function, when required, is served by a finale which deserts the pattern of the preceding variations in favor of a more climactic procedure such as that of a fugue.

The unity implicit in the variation concept appeals to contemporary composers, and at least residual traces of all variation types exist in twentieth-century music.

Multimovement Forms

Individual forms are combined in multimovement forms. Pairs of dances were joined at an early date. These were forerunners of the baroque *suites* and *partitas* which consisted of a group of dance movements in contrasting tempos and styles. The choice and sequence of movements were not completely standardized, but the most prevalent arrangement had an *allemande, courante, sarabande,* and *gigue* in that order. An optional group was often inserted between the sarabande and the gigue, and variously titled preludes somtimes preceded the allemandes. The movements were usually in the same key, but the opposite mode both parallel and relative was sometimes used. Twentieth-century dance suites are descendants of the dance pairs and baroque suites, though none of the earlier conventions are still observed.

Serenade, cassation, and *divertimento* are multimovement types which flourished during the classic era. All three terms are applied to multimovement works for various instrumental combinations. Beyond this, little in the way of uniform criteria can be detected in the various examples of these forms. They are the models followed by the modern suites comprised of assorted movements which do not conform to any preexistent plan. The movements for such suites are often taken from dramatic works—ballets, operas, and motion picture scores. Suites excerpted from dramatic works make appropriate sections of the complete composition available for concert performances.

Unlike suites, which may have any number of movements in random order, *complete sonatas* adhere to uniform standards firmly established by tradition. Symphonies, sonatas, trios, quartets, and all similar works are cast in complete sonata form. Only the mediums are different.

A classic complete sonata form consists of three or four movements. The first is in sonata form and has a fast tempo. The second is a slow movement. Broad ternary, sonata, and variation forms are common. The third movement of four-movement sonatas originally was a minuet and trio, but starting with Beethoven a scherzo often replaces the minuet. The fourth movement is a sonata or rondo form in a fast tempo. When the first movement is only moderately fast, the order of the two middle movements is sometimes reversed. The finale follows the slow movement when there are only three, which is typical in concertos. The second and third movements of concertos frequently are joined or played without interruption, a practice which also occurs in works for other mediums.

The traditional key relationships in complete sonata form are tonic for the fast movements, including minuets and scherzos, and subdominant for the slow movement. Exceptions appeared almost from the beginning, and even token compliance vanished before the present century.

No thematic relationship between movements is expected, but since Beethoven's time common elements have been incorporated in different movements as overall unifying devices. When the sharing of common thematic material between movements is systematic, a *cyclic form* results.

Vocal Forms

Form in vocal music is achieved in the same manner as in instrumental music, that is, by various patterns of repetition. Most if not all of the instrumental forms have vocal counterparts. Many texts are adaptable to simple one-part, binary, and ternary settings, and these forms are sometimes known as *song forms*. The minuet and trio form and *da capo aria* have much in common. The earliest known canons and rounds are for voices, and there are many vocal fugues and fugatos. Sonata and rondo forms are possible but not usual in vocal works. In addition, two types of songs—*strophic* and *through-composed*—have designs peculiar to vocal music.

In a strophic song all of the stanzas of a poem are sung to the same music. This type of setting is appropriate only for poems which have uniform stanzas and a relatively constant mood. It is usual for folk and children's songs and is found in many art songs as well.

The antithesis of a strophic setting is a through-composed setting. The music in a through-composed song is an outgrowth of the text and independent of any abstract musical design. This does not preclude the use of unifying devices such as motives and accompaniment figures, but they are subservient to the text. On a larger scale, operas and oratorios are through-composed in the sense that the sequence of musical events is determined largely by the plot and the text, though internal sections may fit in familiar patterns. One purpose of *leitmotivs* is to provide a unifying device independent of sectional repetitions.

Each text presents special problems in form and suggests unique solutions. For this reason structral stereotypes in vocal music result mostly from bending texts (by way of spurious repetitions) to comply with preconceived abstract patterns such as that of the da capo aria. The former proclivity of composers for instrumental forms in vocal music was perhaps the result of conditioning. In contemporary vocal writing the form as a rule springs from the text, and the literary and musical ideas shape the form rather than vice versa. Ideally, each work both vocal and instrumental creates its own form.

Program and Dramatic Music

Program music was prominent in the early part of this century. It became insignificant while neoclassicism and serialism were ascendant, but descriptive titles at least are once again in vogue. Program music stands in somewhat the same relationship to its program as vocal music does to its text. Literary or pictorial allusions may dictate the chain of musical events or be subordinate to purely musical considerations. The most successful program pieces seem to be those that satisfy the requirements for abstract musical organization and merely offer listeners a program or colorful title as a fillip. Further generalizations about a category which is so nebulous are futile.

Also futile are generalizations about form in dramatic music—operas, ballets, and background music for motion pictures and plays. Each work is unique. Composers with a good command of abstract musical organization are equipped to satisfy the structural requirements of dramatic music, which on the whole are less demanding because of the visual aspects of the production. Listeners are rarely conscious of musical form in dramatic works because their attention is focused on, one could say distracted by, the other elements.

Contemporary Adaptations

The endurance of traditional musical forms through changing periods and styles attests to their adaptability and their validity. The concepts embodied in traditional forms, adjusted to twentieth-century resources and requirements, persist to the present time. Certain trends are evident in the tailoring of conventional forms to contemporary materials and tastes.

The role of tonality has changed drastically. Once a dominant unifying force and source of variety, its influence diminishes when the tonality is vague or ambiguous and disappears when atonality is approached. In music with well-defined tonal centers tonality functions now as always, but remote tonal relationships are exploited both for their own sake and as features of the structure in twentieth-century music.

Reflecting no doubt the rush of modern living, contemporary composers present their ideas tersely. Brevity is venerated. It is achieved not by reducing the content but by eliminating the unessential and tautological. Literal repetitions are scarce, and extended modulatory transitions are unnecessary when abrupt shifts in tonality are commonplace. The succinct succession of ideas requires the concentrated attention of listeners, and composers operate on the premise that attentive listening will prevail. That their optimism is not always justified has not yet led to widespread compromise on this issue.

A high degree of coherence is typical of twentieth-century composition. The exploration of brief, flexible motives, often with a prominent rhythmic element, contributes substantially to logical integration. Freedom in forming vertical and linear associations and revived emphasis on contrapuntal procedures facilitates the manipulation of motives.

One modification of standard forms has been used sufficiently to achieve independent status and have a name—*arch form*. It results from reversing the order of the themes in the recapitulation of sonata forms. This form is represented schematically by the letters A B C D C B A, with A, B, and C as the thematic elements and D as the development section. Sometimes only the order of the first and second themes is reversed, and the principle is applicable with fewer parts, A B C B A. The middle section may be new material, and it probably will be in five-part arch forms. It should be noted that an A B A form exhibits on a small scale the mirroring of themes on either side of a central point characteristic of arch forms. Bartok was a leading exponent of arch form.

The meaning of the term *symphony* has been extended to include vocal compositions and works for orchestra satisfying few of the conditions of the classic form. Of particular interest are symphonies in one movement. Examples are quoted from the one-movement symphonies of Sibelius, Barber, and Harris. There are not enough of them yet to establish a pattern, but they are spawned by the urge to create a more highly unified symphonic work of major proportions than is attainable with the conventional multimovement plan—the same motivating force that led to cyclic symphonies. The one-movement symphony appears as a twentieth-century solution to a perennial problem. In a one-movement symphony the elements of three or four movements may be compressed into a single movement, or the porportions of a single sonata form may be expanded to become a full symphony.

The twelve-tone system in all probability has had the greatest impact on musical organization of all the twentieth-century innovations. The series itself is both a structural element and a tonality surrogate. Twelve-tone music can be written in any of the traditional forms, or the large dimensions of the structure can be generated, like the small ones, by the series. This aspect of twelve-tone organization is touched upon in Chapters 14 and 15. Krenek's *Twelve Short Piano Pieces* (G. Schirmer, 1939) provide an example of a systematic series arrangement. The four forms of one series are introduced and combined in the twelve otherwise independent pieces according to the following scheme:

1. O
2. I
3. R
4. RI
5. O and I
6. O and R
7. O and RI
8. I and R
9. I and RI
10. O, R, and RI
11. O, I, and R
12. O, I, R, and RI

The possibilities for systematic arrangements of the pitch series are unlimited when all 48 forms in the set-complex are available. Systematic ordering of the series forms is the rule when serial control is extended to other parameters of the music as it is in total organization.

Familiarity with the structural plans that composers of the past and present have found most useful is essential as a point of departure, but knowing and using them is no assurance of successful organization. Conceiving the form of a composition is as much a part of the creative process as conceiving the themes, and just as important. The composer's quest for the perfect shape and ideal content is eternal.

Index